Pryor Convictions
and Other Life Sentences

Richard Pryor

with Todd Gold

BOOKS

REVOLVER BOOKS
Second Edition
Published by Revolver Books © 2006, a division of Revolver Entertainment Ltd
PO Box 31643
London W11 2XS, UK
www.revolverbooks.com

Printed in the UK

A CIP Catalogue record for this book is available from the British Library

ISBN: 0 9549407 4 1

Cover design © Revolver Entertainment
Text design and typesetting by Dexter Haven Associates Ltd, London
Printed and bound in Great Britain by Mackays of Chatham Ltd

To my angels

Contents

Acknowledgements

THERE ARE SO MANY PEOPLE WHO HAVE ASSUMED IMPORTANT roles in my life. Some are mentioned in this book. Others are not. However, my thanks and appreciation go out to the entire group. It has been quite a ride. Without you, I might not have become me.

Likewise, I was fortunate in the help I received in preparing this book, which so many people bet I would never finish. Alas, here it is, and in that respect I am grateful to my co-writer Todd Gold; my William Morris agent Dan Strone; my dear friend (let's leave it at that, there's more later) Jennifer Lee; and my co-hort in living life to its funniest, Paul Mooney.

For their assistance, prodding, cajoling, and intractability in various roles over the past few years, I feel obliged to mention David Schumacher; my lawyers, doctors, and accountants; and my physical therapists. There are also my ex-wives, girlfriends, and all my children.

My love goes out to all of you.

PART 1

Introduction

IF WE WERE SITTIN' 'CROSS FROM EACH OTHER RIGHT NOW, YOUR EARS would be filled with a muddy old voice that sounds somethin' between a preacher's Sunday mornin' sermonizin' and a grizzled seen-it-all coot sittin' at a bar drinkin' and spinnin' some wild bullshit, and you know what?

That voice would belong to me.

Mudbone.

I was born in Tupelo, Mississippi. Long time ago. So long ago it ain't worth rememberin' when exactly, because after a certain while, it's just a long time. Now in that time I met some of the most fascinatin' people ever alive, most of whom you've never heard of. But they was fascinatin'. Trust me. There was a lady I met in St. Louis who liked to...

Well, she was fascinatin'. You're just going to have to take my word for it.

The young man who's writin' this book is the most fascinatin' person I ever become acquainted with. He started listenin' to Mudbone back when both of us needed to be reminded that old people weren't no fools.

"Don't get to be old being no fool," I said. "Lot of young wise men deader than a motherfucker."

It tickles my ass just to think Richard Pryor is still around, because he is the motherfucker. Made almost forty movies. Had his name on twenty-five comedy albums, some of which he actually got paid for.

3

People have gone and wrote books about him. College professors include him in lectures. There was even a television special honoring him for being inspirational and shit. But I know the real shit on the motherfucker. Shit, I know Richard since he was a skinny-ass motherfucker—back in Peoria —shooin' flies off his sweaty face at the slaughterhouse, and dreamin' about having a pension and some pussy. But probably not in that order. And then later on, I still knew Richard better than anyone when he fucked up, which about everyone also knows about. Right?

Remember when he fucked up? That fire got on his ass and it fucked him up upstairs. Fried what little brains he had.

Course that's nothin' compared to what's happened since then. A while back he had a heart attack. Then he had what doctors called a quadruple bypass, which is an operation rather than what he should've done for some of his wives.

Bypassed 'em.

And nowadays he's got this MS—multiple sclerosis. Which is a very complicated disease. It don't kill you, though.

It just makes you wish you were dead.

Like some of the womens he's been with. Six marriages to five women. Numerous womens in between. Some at the same time. A revolving door of bitches all come just so he could fuck up their lives and they could fuck up his.

I asked why.

"Because when God makes a fool, he makes a perfect one," he said.

No, seriously.

"Boy, why in the hell don't you just stick with one pussy? Why you gotta go and marry all them bitches? You even married one of 'em twice."

You know what he said to me?

He said, "Shit, I'm just tryin' to find one that'll fit." THAT'S RICHARD. Some people fall in love. Others fall in shit. Richard once said they're the same thing. Oh well, no question the boy is funny. Funny like Ali could fight. The heavyweight champ of hilarity. No doubt about that. I remember the motherfucker back when he was young and truly ignorant. Absolutely nobody was funnier. He could make a motherfucker laugh at a funeral on Sunday, Christmas Day.

Course, that was then. I speak to the boy all the time and I asked him what happened since.

"Monies," he told me. "I got me some monies."

That's what happened to him. He got some monies, and all of a sudden those missed-meal cramps and shit disappeared and he said, "Fuck it."

That's what he told me, anyway.

"Fuck it. I said, 'Fuck it.'"

As for me, I could never afford to say fuck it the way he said it. That's why ol' Mudbone's still hungry. Shit. I've been around so long —long enough that nobody remembers when I started in show business—that I knowed pretty near everybody. Don't mean I liked 'em. I knowed 'em. Big difference. I gave Moms Mabley, who I liked, her break. Moms was an ugly child, and I told her, "Girl, you ought to go into comedy."

Unlike Moms, Richard wasn't ugly. He was just ignorant.

Shit, he didn't even know he was black. Used to call himself Sun. Sun the Secret Prince.

But I told him the same thing as Moms. Go into comedy.

See, I didn't know if he was even listenin'. 'Cause even then you couldn't let him get none of that pot in him. Then it was actually like tryin' to talk to a baboon's ass. I mean, I once talked to him for seven days and seven nights and he was still on the same subject—"Where can I get some more?"

I said, "Boy, why'n't you do something with yourself."

"Like what?"

"Since religion ain't your thing, maybe you can try ballet. You're gonna be black for a long time. So you might as well enjoy yourself. Because there ain't many black motherfuckers doing the ballet."

And then he said, "What about comedy?"

This, of course, reminded me of Moms. For here was another opportunity to start another career.

"What's that like?" he asked.

NOT EASY.

See I was honest with the motherfucker. I told him comedy—real comedy—wasn't only tellin' jokes. It was about telling the truth. Talking about life. Makin' light of the hard times.

"Definitely not as funny as it looks," I said. "You start telling the truth to people and people gonna look at you like you was askin' to fuck their mama or somethin'. The truth is gonna be funny, but it's gonna scare the shit outta folks.

"And maybe you, too."

In any event, the boy was still interested. I could see that much. So I went on. Told him the truth about how I'd lived through hard times.

I said, "People talk about how these are hard times. But hard times was way back. They didn't even have a year for it. Just called it Hard Times.

"And it was dark all the time. I think the sun came out on Wednesday, and if you didn't have your ass up early, you missed it.

"So I happened to be out there one Wednesday and the sun hit me right in the face. I grabbed a bunch of it and rubbed it all over myself. Shit, I didn't have nothing else. And I said, 'Shit, I might as well have some sun on my face.'

"Time went on and I remembered it was Thursday, and because there was no one else around, I said to myself, 'Damn, that sun was a bitch.

That's why they didn't want us to have any of it. 'Cuz it'll cheer you up inside.'"

Needless to say, this made quite a bit of sense to young Rich, who didn't have no sunshine in his life back in Peoria but, in fact, recognized that he might be able to grab some if he went into comedy. Steppin' on stage, bein' in front of the hot spotlight, hearin' the applause and whatnot. The whatnot, of course, bein' all the pussy he knew he'd get as well. It was a risk, a big risk, which he knew.

That sun can get so hot it'll fry your ass like two eggs in a skillet.

But…

But I'm getting ahead of the story, and there's plenty of that to go around.

SEE, not too long ago, I asked him, "After all this, why you want to go and write a book, and especially a book about you? Ain't livin' enough? Ain't survivin' been hard enough? You're the motherfucker. You did it all and it ain't all pretty."

He said, "I know."

So I said, "Then why you want to tell it all again. What good do you think that'll do?"

"Besides make me some monies?" he asked.

"Shit. Of course, besides that."

He said, "It's like this. You didn't have to come to this motherfucker, and you sure can't choose how to leave. You don't even know when you're going to go. So don't take this shit serious. All you can do is have fun and you better have plenty of it, which I did."

"No question about that," I said. "But do you remember it?"

He said, "I remember what's mine."

Shit, you can't argue with that. And what the motherfucker don't remember, I might.

Then I said, "Now what all are you gonna write about? Where you gonna start?"

He laughed. You know how he laughs. Then he lit a cigarette and took a long puff, and that's when I know'd that he'd learned somethin' through all the shit he'd been through. Acquired wisdom. Done become a philosopher.

He said, "There ain't but two pieces of pussy you gonna get in your life. That's your first and your last. All that shit in between—that's just the extra gravy. And that's what I'm gonna write about. The gravy."

Yes, sir. Sounded good to me.

But since I've knowed the motherfucker for so long, and I also know the story, I had but one piece of advice for him.

He asked, "What?"

And I said, "Keep some sunshine on your face."

"I'll try," he said. "I'll try."

1

TO EVERYONE FROM FANS TO WIVES, I WOULD ALWAYS BE A DARK comic genius, the Bard of Self-Destruction, but in the summer of 1986 I literally saw the light, and if that didn't change who I was, it certainly transformed my life. It was the middle of the night. Lying in bed beside my ex-wife Deboragh in my house at Hana, on the island of Maui, Hawaii, I watched shards of light explode across my field of vision as if I was standing in an empty field during a lightning storm.

I didn't know what to make of it. I stared at the lights a long time. They didn't entertain me. Nor did they scare me. I thought I was onto something unique. Then I woke up Deboragh to tell her about it.

"What are you talking about, your theory of light?" she said, unamused and tired.

"Can't you see it?" I said.

"No," she said.

"There!" I exclaimed, pointing at another bolt spearing the darkness. "There! Right there, goddamn it."

Two months later I sat on an airplane, heading to the Mayo Clinic in Rochester, Minnesota. Deboragh sat beside me, as if to prevent my escape. Not that I could've gone anywhere at thirty-five thousand feet, though, I admit, the thought did cross my mind. Death had knocked on my door before. Bullets had just missed me. Womens had gone for my heart, and worse—my balls. I had even set myself on fire and suffered third-degree burns over 50 percent of my body in 1980.

But the stuff that'd been happening lately scared the shit out of me.

It was as if Death had returned for a visit.

"Hey, Rich, remember me?"

"No."

"Rich, why you want to hurt my feelings like that?"

"Get the fuck away, motherfucker."

"HA-HA-HA-HA-HA-HA!"

After seeing the flashing lights in Hawaii, weird shit snuck up on me without warning. My feet went numb. My hands went numb. My fingers didn't do what I told them. My neck went stiff. (Needless to say, if some part of my body was going to stiffen, I preferred it to be my dick.) Suddenly, I couldn't move. Shit would last for a moment or two and then I'd go, "What the fuck was that about?"

Then I'd hear the laughter.

"HA-HA-HA-HA-HA-HA!"

"What was that?"

"Hey, Rich, you remember me now?"

As soon as I began worrying for real that my body was becoming more unreliable than my mind, I saw a doctor at UCLA. The UCLA doc put me through tests and then sent my ass to the Mayo Clinic, where I was poked and prodded as if I was an experiment in Dr. Frankenstein's lab. I mean, shit, they X-rayed me, they tested my reflexes, they put me on a contraption that turned me around like a piece of meat on a rotisserie and shot me and stuck me and drew things out of my poor, confused body.

And they were so casual about it.

"Good morning, Mr. Pryor, and how are you? Today we're going to be taking samples of your blood, shit, and piss. Have a good one."

You ever try to piss in them bottles? There's something too clean about pissing in those bottles. Your dick don't want to do it. I mean, your dick looks at it and says, "Why I gotta piss in this? Well, I ain't gonna do it. You take me over to the toilet where I used to piss. I don't want to piss in the sink."

You say, "Piss, man, please. I'll never be able to leave if you don't."

Finally, if you do start, you can't stop.

"Nurse! I need another bottle! Quick!"

You lose your pride real quick in hospitals. During one test, a doctor stuck a long tube down my ass. No matter what you do to an asshole, it's still an asshole. Ain't going to get any prettier. So there I was, having an intimate relationship with this damn machine, when I turned my head to the side and saw a handful of doctors in the doorway, looking at me. Nothing I could do but turn back to the business.

"Please, Doc, back there," I said. "Them faces."

Nobody stirred.

I asked, "What am I? The treat for the day?"

I'm sure they went home that night and when their wives asked if anything exciting happened at work, they said, "Yeah, I looked up Richard Pryor's asshole."

After a week of intensive, scary, and sometimes humiliating tests, the doctors finished. Seated in one of the main docs' diploma-filled office, I was told the diagnosis. It turned out to be worse than all the tests.

"Mr. Pryor, you have multiple sclerosis."

"Hey, Rich, remember me?"

Oh, shit. I knew who it was this time. No use pretending. Death was back. He sounded like Jim Brown on steroids.

"Am I gonna die?"

"Naw, not yet. I'm just gonna fuck with you for a while. HA-HA-HA-HA!"

You know how sometimes you're too stupid to be frightened when that's really the way you should be acting? Well, I was both stupid and frightened. I didn't know what the fuck the doctor meant when he informed me that I had multiple sclerosis. Nor did I want to know. Deboragh and I went straight back to the hotel, packed, and caught the first available plane back to L.A. I don't think we mentioned MS once.

But eight years have passed since that fateful day in Rochester, and now I know more about MS than some doctors. MS is a strange and, thus far, incurable, degenerative disease that attacks the protective sheath around the nerve fibers. They say it affects motor skills, balance, and simple involuntary acts such as swallowing. But it doesn't merely affect them, it takes them the fuck away.

People call me all the time and say, "Richard, I heard you were dead."

"What do you think?" I reply. "You're talking to me. Does that help?"

I know what they're talking about, though. MS makes you feel like a decoy in a shooting gallery for self-pity and depression. In my mind, I've written the obituary countless newspaper men have had waiting for years. RICHARD PRYOR DIES. But instead of the cause being drugs or a heart attack or an angry woman, as most would've expected, MS has added a punch line.

"Pryor died when he fell down and couldn't get up."

I'd be lying if I didn't admit there've been many days when I wanted to pick up the .357 beside my bed and drop the curtain. Call it a show. But I've never taken the easy way. Even when it seemed easy, it wasn't easy. Why, I don't know. That's just the way it's been. Black man's fate, I suppose.

So rather than surrender to forces beyond my control, I've decided to hang on till the end of the ride. See where the motherfucker takes me. I've had similar experiences with women. I mean, you know the bitch is going to be trouble, but you still can't help yourself.

The brain says, "Get the pussy, get the pussy," and you can't do nothing else.

◆   ◆   ◆

I've found that my life, instead of ending because of MS, has only changed. Perhaps it was God's way of telling me to chill, slow down, look at the trees, sniff the flowers rather than the coke, and take time for myself and see what it's like to be a human being. See what it's like being human.

I lived big for a time, but never appreciated life. I never realized that people really liked me.

Mr. Richard Pryor, a human being.

But like I said, that's all changed since I became ill. I've been surprised and deeply touched by people in more ways than I could've imagined. We're still years away from any sort of cure for multiple sclerosis, but I'm able to make do. I look in the mirror. I know that's me looking back at me.

"Hey, Rich, how you doin'?"

"Above ground."

This is my life. I know the truth. If you ain't here, you're nowhere. So, I go on, because it ain't over. Only stranger.

Shit.

Who would've ever guessed I'd make it this far?

2

I NEVER THOUGHT I HAD A SELF-DESTRUCT MECHANISM WORKING inside of me, but considering the way things worked out, I see I caused most of the problems myself. It was always plain to other people, I suppose. When I was a kid, my grandfather and uncle bet that I wouldn't make it to fourteen. Even I figured the chances of me making it to twenty were slim.

That's sad, betting against yourself.

Why didn't you see that then, Rich?

Sometimes survival depends on blindness. After living on this planet for sixty-five years, I realize that my entire life might've been decided when I was five years old. Imagine that. Going about business for sixty years, searching for the key that'll unlock all the answers, and then finding out it happened way back.

That's what people mean when they say life is funny.

I wasn't much taller than my daddy's shin when I found that I could make my family laugh. It happened outside the house at 313 North Washington, in Peoria, Illinois, where I lived among an assortment of relatives, neighbors, whores, and winos—the people who inspired a lifetime of comedic material.

I was a skinny little black kid, with big eyes that took in the whole world and a wide, bright smile that begged for more attention than anybody had time to give. Dressed in a cowboy outfit—the only range rustler in all of Peoria—I sat on a railing of bricks and found that when I fell off on purpose everyone laughed, including my grandmother, who made it her job to scare the shit out of people.

From that first pratfall, I liked being the source of making people laugh. After a few more minutes of falling, a little dog wandered by and pooh-poohed in our yard. I got up, ran to my grandmother, and slipped in the dog poop. It made Mama and the rest laugh again. Shit, I was really onto something then. So I did it a second time.

"Look at that boy! He's crazy!"

That was my first joke.

All in shit.

And I been covered in it ever since.

I spent the first twenty-one years of my life in Peoria.

They called Peoria the model city. That meant they had the niggers under control.

Black people didn't have it so good in Peoria. If they worked at all, they were probably employed at one of the nearby slaughterhouses. My family dodged that fate. They ran whorehouses, bars, drove trucks, and shit. But the fact was, almost half the black people living in Peoria's ghetto didn't have any job whatsoever. Only two restaurants and two movie theaters in town served people of color, and if a black man wanted a hotel room for the night, he had to find it elsewhere.

We had a curfew in my neighborhood. Niggers home by eleven. Negroes by midnight.

That was the reality. But childhood is colored by ignorance, a good ignorance, one that leads you around in a blindness necessary for survival. Even the best of days in Peoria were tainted by gloom, a murky darkness that hung over people the same way smog lays flat over a city as pretty as L.A. It just fucks up the picture. I saw shit that would cause an adult nightmares. Heard tales about hangings and murders that happened just because a man happened to be black. Strange shit.

I didn't understand it.

"Didn't you know you were black?"

"Shit, I didn't even know I had a color."

I never wanted to be white. I always wanted to be something different than a nigger, because niggers had it so rough. I tried to be a black cat with neat hair. I thought that was the problem—the hair.

In my imagination, I gave myself a new identity. I called myself Sun the Secret Prince. As Sun the Secret Prince, I was colorless. I was just light and energy, caroming off the planets. No boundaries. Simply alive.

Then one day my grandmother brought me down to earth. Told me I was black.

Said, "Boy, you're black."

Okay, Grandma. I see that. But I still didn't understand the things that went with being black. That came later.

I was being prepared, though. The movies fucked me up. So did television. I watched shows like "Father Knows Best" and believed that was how everybody in America lived. But my family didn't resemble them one bit.

White folks do things a lot different than niggers. They eat quieter. "Pass the potatoes. Thank you, darling. Could I have a bit of that sauce? How are the kids coming along with their studies? Think we'll be having sexual intercourse this evening? We're not? Well, what the heck."

Black families be different. When my father ate, he made noise. "Hey, bitch, where's the food? Goddamn, Mama, come on. Shit. Come on, motherfucker, can't you make that meat stick to the bone."

White folks fuck quiet, too. I've seen it in the movies. "Ou, boop, eh, boo."

Niggers make noise. "Oh, you motherfucker. Oh, goddamn, baby. Oh, don't lose that thing."

So if I wasn't like those people on TV, what did that make me? Where did I fit in?

Those were the questions I often asked myself, and continued to do so my entire life. But there were others I never got a chance to ask. Like those concerning my family's background. As far as I could tell, my people had been around since the beginning of time, like Adam and Eve. They just were. Despite a natural curiosity about those origins, I didn't want to upset anyone by asking questions they'd consider nonsense—not to mention a waste of time.

I didn't want to hear that familiar refrain, "Child, can't you see I'm busy!"

No one was busier than my grandmother, Marie Carter. She reminded me of a large sunflower—big, strong, bright, appealing. But Mama, as I also called her, was also a mean, tough, controlling bitch. One of twenty-one children, she was born in Decatur, Illinois, and grew up knowing terrible prejudice. The kind of shit that adults didn't have to speak about because they all knew. It was in their eyes. Rage, fear, wariness. Once I overheard her talking about a black man who was lynched by the Ku Klux Klan.

"Why, Mama?" I asked.

"'Cuz he was a nigger."

I thought about that hard. Tried to understand why something like that happened.

You don't forget that shit.

"Am I gonna get hanged, Mama?"

"Go and play, boy."

LeRoy Pryor must've been some specimen. It's impossible to know whether or not Marie ever married him, but they had four children together. After the last child was born in the late 1920s, LeRoy went off to work on the railroad. Though he planned on being gone only a short time, he got buckled between two trains. The collision should've killed him instantly. But when the trains parted, he stepped out and walked to a nearby tavern.

Man wanted a drink. And then he died.

Bless his soul.

I hope I have some of that strength inside me.

In 1929, Marie packed up her children and belongings and moved to Peoria, where she met Thomas Bryant. I would call him Pops. Like Marie, he was a hodgepodge of heritage, including part Native American. In fact, he was raised on a reservation, but left at age nine, preferring the road over family.

"Why'd you leave the reservation, Pops?" I asked.

As a boy, I was fascinated by cowboys and Indians and couldn't imagine leaving an actual reservation.

"'Cuz people used to squat and shit," he said. "Right there in the dirt. It wasn't nice."

Pops and Marie made quite a picture. He was a conservative Democrat who believed in America and the law. Marie was a beautiful young woman with hustle in her bloodstream. Pops was ten years older than her, a man with itchy britches. He roamed. Marie had four kids who anchored her in one place. But instead of running the other way, Pops told Marie that he liked her so much he'd take care of her family.

"That's strange for a young man," I once remarked.

"It's different," he replied.

So were they. Although married for something like forty or fifty years, Pops and Marie barely exchanged a single word. They quit speaking after she caught him fucking one of her whores. Rather than throw his ass out of the house, Marie did worse. She defied Pops to ever have another woman. Any woman other than her. Know what I mean? She fucked his head up good.

From what I could tell, Pops didn't mind not talking to Marie for most of their married life. He swore that his real punishment was having to sleep with me after Marie threw him out of their room. I used to roll and toss all over the bed. Pops said I was the kickingest motherfucker he'd ever met in his life. Couldn't sleep with either Marie or me. Bless his heart.

Then there was LeRoy Jr., my father. He was better known as Buck Carter. Big and strong, he was a Golden Gloves boxing champion as a teenager. Later, he traveled from Chicago to East St. Louis, working odd jobs until he got the urge to move on again. The girl he finally took up with, Gertrude Thomas, lived in the same neighborhood as Marie and Pops. Gertrude was a bookkeeper. Not to mention trouble.

I know that Buck loved her. For real. He felt that deep kind of love that doesn't ever do a person good, that ends up kicking you in the ass, leaving you crying and tormented. Years later, Buck admitted that he was glad Gertrude had gone. He loved her so much, he said he probably would've killed her.

Buck and Gertrude were involved—as were some of the other Carters, Bryants, Pryors, and Thomases in Peoria—in operating the whorehouses and bars that gave the Washington Street area its reputation. I know my mother didn't expect to get pregnant. Nor did she want the baby who arrived on December 1, 1940.

Or so they told me.

But the circumstances surrounding my birth seem obvious. My dad wanted the pussy. My mother had the pussy. Nine months later, my Uncle Franklin had a premonition about seeing a baby in a manger. And then I arrived.

At least Gertrude didn't flush me down the toilet as some did. When I was a kid, I found a baby in a shoe box—dead. An accident to some, I was luckier than others, and that was just the way it was.

I don't know where my mother got the name Richard. Franklin, though, was my uncle's.

Richard Franklin.

The next one, Lennox, was one of my aunt's boyfriends.

Richard Franklin Lennox.

Thomas was her maiden name, and Pryor was my maiden name.

Richard Franklin Lennox Thomas Pryor.

I wish I would've asked my mother more about how I came to be, but I didn't. Why didn't you, Richard?

Gertrude drank a lot. She'd be home for six months or so, and then one day she'd leave the house as if she was going to the store, say goodbye and be gone for six months. How did that make you feel, Richard?

My dad always seemed to know when Gertrude was about to take off and it didn't bother him any that I could tell. But I just thought it was nice to see her whenever she was at home. I didn't want to upset her by asking any questions.

You know?

She was my mom.

I didn't want to shake up shit.

3

FROM MY EARLIEST DAYS, I LEARNED THAT EXPECTATIONS HAD TO be balanced against reality. Take the first Christmas I remember clearly. I was two years old, standing up in my crib, staring at the multicolored lights on the Christmas tree. I realized it was a special time of year. The decorations on the tree added a brightness that wasn't normally part of the house, and the presents under it were even better because some of them belonged to me.

As I plotted my escape from behind bars, my cousin Martha came in the room. She was my Aunt Dee's daughter. She was also my chance to fly out of that crib.

"Hey, bitch, lift my ass out of here," I wanted to say, but at that age the only thing I managed to do was lean against the railing of the crib, making funny sounds, and look at her with my friendly wide eyes. Maybe Martha would help me out. Let me get at those presents. I could only hope.

But you know what happened?

Martha vomited on me.

She did. Bless her heart. She was drunk.

Family is a mixed blessing. You're glad to have one, but it's also like receiving a life sentence for a crime you didn't commit. My people had a variety of last names—Carter, Bryant, Thomas, and Pryor. They were an industrious, busy group. My grandma and mother ran houses. My father and uncle helped at Pop's bar, the Famous Door. There was also a trucking business, a beauty parlor, and so on. Anything to stay afloat.

My Aunt Dee and Uncle Dickie were prime examples. She came to Peoria from Mississippi and nabbed Dickie in his youth, married him, and then turned him out. Made him a pimp. I don't blame him, though. He didn't know nothing.

Later, Dickie took over tending bar at the Famous Door when my dad went in the service, but it always seemed to me his main occupation—the one he preferred—was getting me in trouble. One time my grandma called down to 317 North Washington. I picked up the phone. She wanted Dickie, but he squatted in the background and put words in my head as if he was a bad conscience.

"Tell her she ain't the fat hen's ass," he whispered and then laughed.

"Hey, Grandma, you ain't the fat hen's ass."

She said, "I'll be right there, son," and then a few minutes later, she showed up and whacked me with a belt. Made me holler and tell the truth.

"I promise. I ain't ever gonna say you ain't the fat hen's ass no more."

Whack! Whomp! Whack!

"Damn right you aren't."

What she should've done is beat the crap out of Dickie. But he'd disappeared, leaving me to catch her wrath.

The house where I grew up at 317 North Washington had a strange, dark, big feel. It stood amid whole blocks of such places. In between were various businesses—a trucking office across the street; further down was a parking lot of semitrailers; a garage; liquor stores.

I lived in a neighborhood with a lot of whorehouses. Not many candy stores or banks. Liquor stores and whorehouses. Niggers love to drink. They say. White people have banks and shit. But you guys have to go four miles to get some liquor. A nigger can get liquor by walking out the door.

My grandmother's house was at 313. Between hers and ours was China Bee's, where the pretty whores lived. That says something about the whores who worked for my grandma. Didn't seem to matter either way, though. Both places did pretty good.

There was a little vacant patch of dirt down the block from our home, just to the left. A little patch of dirt and grass looking for the countryside. Asking, "Why I got to be in the city? Why can't I have no trees and grass?" For some reason, these giant sunflowers grew in the middle of that patch. I don't know how they got started or who watered them, but every summer they headed up toward the sky as if they were trying to escape the ghetto. After realizing they couldn't get out, they bloomed. Big. Like giant sunbursts. I loved those flowers, man. Looking at them made me feel good.

One day in 1944, a strange person wearing a soldier's uniform walked into our home as if he owned the place. A little frightened by his sudden appearance, I watched him come inside and puzzled over what he was doing there. Like who the fuck was he? I was used to strangers coming and going, but all of them had business to do. Getting the pussy.

But this guy didn't seem to have anything on his mind except lingering. I watched him go upstairs. A few minutes later, he returned in a different set of clothes and then I recognized him as my father. He'd come back from the Army.

Everybody celebrated, and I had the impression that for those few hours none of the usual hustle and worry mattered. Daddy slipped back into his old job bartending at the Famous Door, where my mom also waitressed in a tight, white dress. I loved how it looked against her velvet tan skin. I thought it made Gertrude look very sexy.

The Famous Door was where I hung out. It was a wild, colorful place for a kid to spend most of his time, but everybody in my family congregated there. The news you picked up there was better than what you got in the paper. I remember Uncle Dickie running in and informing everybody that his friend Shoeshine had murdered his two women in a chicken shack after discovering that they were fucking each other rather than him.

"He took that for real," Dickie said. "Absolutely."

As a comedian, I couldn't have asked for better material. My eyes and ears absorbed everything. People came in to exchange news, blow steam, or have their say. Everybody had an opinion about something. Even if they didn't know shit about sports, politics, women, the war. In fact, the less people knew, the louder they got.

Some niggers used to drink and want to fight. Some drank and had a seizure. Everybody knows some nigger who drinks and every weekend gets his ass whooped. He never wins, but he always wants to fight. Nice guy during the week. "Hi, how ya doing?" But the weekend comes and he's, "Motherfucker, get out of my face."

You see him in the bar and he's fucked up. Starts in, "Man, leave me alone, nigger. Shit, you ain't gonna start fucking with me. Give me some money...

"Nigger give me my whiskey. What? I'm drunk? What you mean I'm drunk motherfucker? You crazy. Shit, you didn't say that an hour ago. When you were serving me that shit and I was buying everybody in here... something. Give me a beer. For everybody. One motherfucking beer."

One night some guy came in and cussed my grandmother. Buck heard it, grabbed a pistol, and shot the man full of bullets. Emptied the magazine. Blam! Blam! Blam! Scared the shit out of everyone in the place. But liquor makes you do strange things. Like not die when you're supposed to. The man was pissed, and he managed to crawl across the floor and cut Buck on his leg. My father was crippled the rest of his life. The other guy showed up for drinks a few months later.

Another night a marine came in and raised hell. Like it was in the movies. Yelling. Throwing shit. Grabbing the women's titties and ass. Dickie and Buck grabbed him and started throwing punches. The three of them fought for a good half hour. But when it was all over, they laughed and drank together.

"Daddy, what's going on?" I asked after some similarly crazy incident at the bar.

He turned around and smacked me.

"Shut up. Don't ask questions."

When you're a little guy watching all this weird shit happen and no one explains it, you formulate your own thoughts. Once I saw some guy who was fighting get knifed in the stomach. With his guts hanging out, he wanted to get to the liquor store down the street. I didn't understand. The dude was screaming for someone to help him down the block. His eyes locked on me.

"Come on, man," I said bravely. "The ambulance is coming. Why don't you just lay there."

He looked at me like I was the crazy one and said, "Shit, I'm going to get me a half pint."

I wondered where he was going to put that half pint. If he drank it, I thought he'd die instantly.

Of course, that's what I thought. But I found out different. Assholes don't die. They multiply.

4

ON SUNDAYS, MY GRANDMOTHER MADE ME GO WITH HER TO THE Morning Star Baptist Church. I didn't want to go, but you didn't fuck around with Marie. You did what she said. After a while, though, I drifted to the Salvation Army Church where I got to beat the collection drum. And when it was somebody's birthday, I got to beat it a few extra times. Made me feel special.

There was lots of talk in my house about God. "Help me, God." "Please God." "Why you doin' this to me, God?" "Goddamn it." Shit like that. And then there were all them Bible stories, which scared the motherfucking crap out of me. They were all horrible stories in which God always managed to do something spectacular at the last minute. Kind of like Superman.

As a result, I learned early on not to fuck with this God guy, this God person.

Every wino knew Jesus. "You know Jesus Christ?"

"Jesus Christ? Shit, lives over there in the projects. Runs the elevator in the Jefferson Hotel. Nigger ain't shit. Neither is his mama."

The only person scarier than God was my mother. Gertrude was a trip. My dad understood this, but I guess he couldn't help himself.

One time Buck hit Gertrude, and she turned blue with anger and said, "Okay, motherfucker, don't hit me no more."

She said that. I give her that.

But I guess Buck didn't care. Standing in his underwear and T-shirt, decked out like an inebriated bedroom heavyweight, he whomped her again.

Mistake.

"Oh no, don't do that," she said, coiling like a rattlesnake about to strike. "Don't stand in front of me with fucking undershorts on and hit me, motherfucker."

Quick as lightning, she reached out with her finger claws and swiped at my father's dick. Ripped his nutsack off.

I was just a kid when I saw this.

My father ran down the street to 313 hollering, "Mama! Mama! Mama!"

A grown man.

I stood outside and saw him running up the block. His shorts were all red with blood.

"What happened, Daddy?"

"She cut my nuts open!"

"Who did?"

"Your bitch-ass mother! Gertrude!"

Traumatized, I wandered back home. Mama stood in the doorway, looking satisfied with herself. She seemed happy to see me.

"Hi, baby," she said, and then she hugged me. Rubbed my head. Confused my ass just by being so nice to me.

But she wasn't nice to my dad that night. Ended his pimpship right then.

The Pryor men know about pain. One afternoon I crawled under the front porch so I could play in the soft dirt. My grandma caught me, gave me a scolding, and then hauled my ass to the bathtub. She washed me off and put on clean clothes. So what did I do next? Went back outside and crawled under the porch. I was happy as a dick in pussy digging in that soft, cool dirt when she stepped out and found me again.

"Oh, so you don't believe fat meat's greasy, do you?" Marie said.

She snatched me up, threw me back into the bath, cleaned me up again, threw on another set of clean clothes, and let me go back outside. Didn't bother me any. I went under the porch just like before and played in the soft dirt, until she busted me again.

"I'm going to beat your ass this time," she said.

Bless her heart. And she beat my ass.

That's just the way it was. As much as I wanted love and attention, I couldn't help but feel that I was a source of hardship for my parents, something they'd as soon forget as let me intrude on their lives. Summer was the worst time. All the men and women went to the Cardinals baseball games in St. Louis. I wanted to go, too. Each time, I got ready and waited by the front door as they came downstairs.

"Look at that boy," my mama said. "Where does he think he's going?"

There was laughter.

"You ain't going," my dad said with finality.

"Oh," I said, lowering my eyes.

After they left, I cried. Not in front of them. Only after they were gone. Only after I pressed my nose to the window and watched their car swing around the corner and out of sight. I knew they didn't hate me. So why didn't they want to take me?

"Why, Grandma?" I once asked.

She looked at me. Then slapped me upside my head.

Growing up was a minefield. I had to watch every step, but it was hard to remember all the time. I was something like six years old when a sick pedophile turned me into a pincushion for his perverted urges. What did I know, though?

I was playing by myself in the alley behind our house, throwing stones at trash cans and scaring rats out from their hiding places and pretending to hunt them.

Suddenly, this older guy appeared from around the corner. He stepped in from the shadows. His name was Hoss. He was in his late teens, probably around sixteen or seventeen. Right away, I knew he was trouble. I saw it in his bloodshot eyes. In no uncertain terms, he said, "I'm gonna fuck with you, you little chickenshit pussy."

I should've run. But I didn't. Because he was right about me in that sense—I was a little chickenshit. It was as if the terror I felt paralyzed me. Glued me in place and made me easy prey. Hoss threw me against the wall in a darkened corner shielded from the view of anyone passing by. Then he unzipped his pants and put his dick into my mouth.

"Suck it," he ordered.

Relieved he didn't want no asshole, I did as told. Afterward, Hoss walked off happy and left me trembling in the chilly darkness. I cried and shook and tried to make sense of what had happened. I knew something horrible had happened to me. I felt violated, humiliated, dirty, fearful, and, most of all, ashamed. But I couldn't sort that shit out. Fuck.

I carried that secret around for most of my life.

I told no one. Ever.

Hoss quit bothering me after a partner of his told him he couldn't do that to me anymore. The same guy also came up to me and said, "Hey, man, you can't suck no dick."

Aw, shit. Somebody else knew. I was humiliated and shamed even more.

Several nights later, I sat at the supper table with my dad and grandmother. In the middle of eating, my dad started singing the song "I'm Forever Blowing Bubbles." I felt a shiver of embarrassment and mortification run up and down my spine like rats in a wall. What the fuck? Did he know, too?

And if he knew, I wondered, why didn't he do something? Why didn't he cut off Hoss's dick?

Then again, maybe it was a coincidence that he sang that song. I don't know why he sang it. I never asked. He never said anything, either. But it sure upset me.

For the rest of my life, I cursed Hoss like no motherfucker's ever been cursed. I even invented new cuss words. Chickenlickingmotherfuckingdickfucker. I beat his ass a million times. I replayed the rape, but in my revamped version I bit his dick off rather than do as he told. I laughed at him. I did everything short of murder him. Because I hated what he did more than anything that had ever happened to me.

The man put his dick in my mouth!

Many years later I went back to Peoria to make *Jo Jo Dancer, Your Life Is Calling* and heard that Hoss was looking for me. Oddly, even though I was a famous and successful comedian, surrounded by big, menacing bodyguards who would've killed at the snap of my fingers, I was seized by that old sense of fear of Hoss telling me to suck his dick.

I thought I'd shaken the memory.

Guess not.

Motherfucker.

Had me a ghost rattling in the attic. It didn't matter that I lived in a big house behind a gate in Los Angeles, some half a country from the bricks and bars of the old neighborhood. My ass was haunted by the image of Hoss's dick.

As I waited for him, I imagined him winking, asking me to go outside and then to suck his dick.

I wondered how to respond.

I thought about killing the motherfucker. Getting even after all these years. But I'm too much of a chickenshit, and I knew, given my luck, that he'd live to testify against me and send my ass to jail. And I knew the kind of dick I'd get there.

Finally, one afternoon Hoss showed up at my trailer. I was curious how he'd look after all these years, but I was more concerned with how I'd respond to him. I didn't know what the fuck to do. I opened the door. Hoss stood there looking older but otherwise not much different than I remembered him. He had a small boy with him. His arm was on the boy's shoulder.

"This is my son," he said, extending his hand toward me as if we were old friends.

I couldn't believe it. After preparing a lifetime for this moment, I suddenly had nothing to say. Nor did Hoss. What was done was done. What was there to do?

"He's a real big fan of yours," Hoss said of his little boy. "I told him I'd bring him down and ask for an autograph."

"Okay," I said.

The boy was about the same age I'd been when his father raped me. I never could forget. I hoped the boy fared better.

5

MY DAD LOVED MY MOM SO MUCH THAT HE WAS FOREVER ASKING himself the question "Why?" That happened to me at the end of several marriages. Sometimes you can't help yourself.

Buck and Gertrude were like that. They had a strange relationship. He was rough, but she talked nasty, disappeared for long, mysterious spells, and when she was around, she drank and argued.

One night Gertrude, as she did so often, said goodbye to my dad and walked out of the house. Only this time she wasn't planning on coming back. She went to her family's farm in Springfield.

Soon after, my grandma had me dress in clothes I only wore to church and then I went with her and my dad to court.

I was ten years old. Not too wise, but savvy enough to know my mom and dad were getting a divorce and that I had to deliver certain lines at the custody hearing. My grandmother said, "Don't be nervous now. When the judge asks you who you want to live with, you say me. All right?"

I wanted to know more about why my mother wasn't coming back to stay with us, but I also knew to shrug off what I couldn't understand.

"Yes, Mama," I whispered.

Then the judge did his thing and asked where I wanted to live.

"With her," I said, pointing to Marie. "I'd like to be with my grandma, please."

The judge nodded. There was more discussion. I didn't know if I'd done good or bad. Then my grandmother was made my legal guardian. I still didn't know if I'd done good or bad.

That I remember. I also remember thinking that I broke my mother's heart by denying her that right.

But Ma, I thought they were going to kill me if I said that I wanted to live with you.

Oh, well.

Gertrude stayed a part of my life. Every so often, I packed my suitcase and took the train to Springfield. Half an hour before I arrived, I began staring out the window, looking for her. I was always relieved to see Gertrude standing on the platform. Then she took me back to the farm in her father's car. Once I spent an entire summer on the farm, and recall that time as the happiest of my life.

The farm was paradise, a playground where my imagination could go wild. At night, I listened to crickets instead of creaking beds and moans, and in the morning, I woke to the sound of roosters crowing and the smell of hot biscuits and fresh-brewed coffee. My grandpa, Bob Thomas, allowed me to help with the chores, which gave me a sense of purpose I didn't have at home.

In addition to farming, he drove a garbage truck. He hauled rubbish to the dump he owned next to the farm. That dump was the site of numerous adventures. At night, for instance, I took a .22, wandered down to the dump, pretending that I was a cowboy or soldier, and waited for some big motherfucking rats to come out. Then I opened fire.

Ka-chu! Ka-chu!

Yes, sir, I fucked up some rats.

◆   ◆   ◆

My mother didn't stay single for long. After she remarried, she asked me why I didn't call her new husband "Daddy."

"He's your father," she said. "You call him that or I'll beat your ass."

"But he ain't my daddy," I argued.

That pissed her off even more.

"Well, you call that other woman 'Mom.'"

The other woman was Viola Hurst, and my mother was right about the fact I called her Mom. I don't know why I did that, but my daddy and I were going to see Sugar Ray Robinson fight in Chicago, and on the way he surprised me by stopping next door at China Bee's house to pick up Viola. I watched her get into the car and thought she was very sexy.

"This is my son, Richard," he said.

"Hello there," Viola smiled.

"Hi, Mom," I said.

It's strange I called her that. But the night before, I'd overheard Gertrude tell my dad that she thought I was nuts. I didn't know why she said that. Nor did I ask anyone for an explanation. So many things were impossible to understand that after a certain point you just quit trying. You dealt with the facts, with survival. You didn't trust anybody. You watched your back. You covered your ass. You said whatever you had to to stay out of trouble.

On television, people talk about having happy lives, but in the world in which I grew up, happiness was a moment rather than a state of being. It buzzed around, just out of reach, like Tinkerbell, flirting and teasing and laughing at your ass. It never stayed long enough for you to get to know it good. Just a taste here and there. A kiss, a sniff, a stroke, a snort.

Yet those were the moments I learned to chase.

I remember the first time I had an orgasm. Because when you first started jacking off, you didn't come. You just had that funny feeling.

In fact, the first time I came I thought something was wrong with me. Said to my dick, "Oh, shit, look what you've done to me."

An hour later, I was back, Jack. Asked my dick, "Can you do it again?"

It's only natural for a young boy of ten to think about sex, but living in a whorehouse gave me special access to those mysteries of the flesh that elude most people until they're older. I spied through the keyholes, putting my eye to the little opening every chance I got. I bumped my head a lot, but I also got an education you couldn't get in school.

Once I saw my own mother in bed with a man. White dude. She didn't seem to mind. But it fucked me up.

Tricks used to come through our neighborhood. That's where I first met white people. They came down to our neighborhood and helped the economy. I could've been a bigot, you know what I mean? I could've been prejudiced. I met nice white men. They said, "Hello, little boy. Is your mother home? I'd like a blow job."

I wonder what would happen if niggers went to white neighborhoods doing that shit. "Hey, man, your mama home? Tell the bitch we want to fuck!"

The prostitutes sat in the big picture window and waved to the customers. All sorts. Whites and blacks. Businessmen. Politicians. Junkies. I spent a lot of time sitting with them, yakking, laughing, and bullshitting.

God, there were some characters. Like Mary. She was a real, honest-to-goodness hermaphrodite. Had a pussy *and* a dick. That shit fucked me up. But she didn't mind. People asked what her name was and she said, "They call me Coffee, 'cuz I grind so fine."

I never had nothing to do with her, other than laughing a hell of a lot. She was a funny lady.

But as soon as some guy entered, those womens kicked me out, closed the door and went to work.

It was weird. I remember a white dude used to come down and ask, "Do you have any girls who'll cover you with ice cream? And little boys that'll lick it off?"

And he was the mayor.

They had me run to the store to get them tampons. I cleaned up in the bathrooms and stuff and found all their women shit around. You know? That's when I decided women are nasty motherfuckers. Then my dick came to life. Started thinking for itself. Bossing me around.

I discovered masturbating when I was about nine or ten. I was in the tub and said, "Hey, I'm onto something here. Shit, I bet Dad don't know about this." After that, they couldn't keep my ass out of the tub.

I never got to scootch any of the whores, but they sure made my dick hard. Swear to God.

One time I crawled up into a vent that looked into one of the upstairs rooms, where one of Mama's whores had brought a john. Shit, they attacked each other, humping and pumping with a furiousness I'd never imagined. I got so involved watching him suck her pussy that I took the vent out and stuck my head out into the room.

Tricks would be fucking, right. They'd be, "Oh, oh, God. Golly, ma'am. Is it really good? Is it really good?"

And the whores be going, "Oh, it's good, baby. Oh, goddamnit. Oh, shit. Damn, there ain't nobody like you, baby. Oh, goddamn."

Years later, I got to be with the same prostitute and I told her the story.

"No, I didn't see you, baby," she said.

"I saw you," I smiled mischievously. Then I pointed to the vent. "I was right up there."

She didn't even open her eyes.

"Go ahead, tell me about it, baby, as you suck on my pussy."

Girls mystified me, man. Scared the crap out of me. I don't know, maybe I thought I was ugly or stupid or something.

When I was a teenager, I didn't get nothing from the girls. Some of the cool guys could get something all the time. Remember those guys? They could say "Bitch," and all the girls would melt. I said that and got an ass whoopin'.

I lost my virginity courtesy of Mr. Spinks. Spinks was a local player, a pimp and dealer. He defined the word *jive*. He lived with this beautiful lady named Penny, who reminded me of Ava Gardner and often crept into my horny imagination.

One day I ventured over to their place, knowing that Spinks was out doing his things and that I could have Penny all to myself. I didn't expect to do anything more than talk and do weird, disgusting things to her in my mind. I wasn't alone with her for ten minutes before Penny asked me to do some of that stuff I was thinking about. Feel her titties, grab her ass. As I complied, my dick showed its appreciation. But I didn't know what to do once I got to that point, which was embarrassing.

"You never fucked anyone before, honey?" she asked. "Did you?"

I shook my head no.

Never mind getting into a girl's panties. I'd never been in one's house.

Fathers kicked ass in my neighborhood. They talked to us on the porch. "Say, boy, what's your name? Jenkins? Let me tell you something, boy. You stay away from my house. See, I workst too hard to send my girls to school to get an education, and not the kind you wants to give them. Now if I catch you around here, I'm gonna take this bad leg off and wear your ass out with it."

"Come on over here," Penny said. "I'm gonna show you what they do when the doors are shut."

And she did.

She said, "Just put it in there. Yeah, right there. Now up and down, you now."

I did what she said.

"Yeah, baby," she continued. "Go up and down. Up and down. Don't stop."

She fucked me good.

Afterward, I understood why that man had been on top of my mother.

Getting the pussy just like me.

Then Spinks came home. I was in the bathroom when I heard the door open and close. Then I heard him say hi to Penny. Oh, shit. He wanted to make small talk. He asked what was going on. I listened, my ear to the door as I pulled on the rest of my clothes and wondered how I was going to *get the fuck out*.

But I couldn't move. I was too scared.

"Come on out of there," Spinks said.

Was he talking to me?

Then I heard pounding on the bathroom door.

"Rich, get the hell out of there!"

I didn't say a word.

"Listen, boy. Get the fuck out."

I prepared to get clobbered, maybe even killed. Then I opened the door and braced for the worst. After nothing hit me, I slowly opened my eyes. Spinks and Penny were on the sofa, staring at me. Their grins were the size of Chevys.

The embarrassment I felt then was even worse than not knowing what to do with my boner.

"Hi," I said sheepishly. "Uh, thanks. Uh, I gotta go. See ya."

Thinking about it now, I can see that Spinks probably told her to do that to me. Not that I'm complaining, you know.

6

MY FOLKS GAVE ME A CHANCE AT SOMETHING BETTER BY
putting me in Catholic school, where I thrived. I made friends.
I got straight A's. I showed promise. The teachers were impressed.
They thought I was smart and encouraged me to aim high.
Then someone found out about the family business and that
blew my chance. They gave me the boot. Kicked my ass out into
the cold.

I was crushed by this inexplicable rejection by people who
professed love and forgiveness.

"Why'd they kick me out of school?" I asked my grandma.
"What did I do?"

"Nothing, baby," she said. "Some people just don't know right
from wrong, even though they think they wrote the book."

Mama left it to me to discover that the world overflowed with
hypocrisy, and it didn't take long. Despite being expelled from
Catholic school, I was forced by my stepmother to continue going
to catechism on weekends. One Saturday a priest came on to me
like a girlfriend. He snuck up on me and gave me a smooch on the
lips. I ran home, bawling and heaving the whole way but especially
hard as I told and retold the story.

"See, I was in church," I explained. "And the guy there gave me some smooches."

"Where?" my daddy asked.

"On the lips."

"Where were you?" my Uncle Dickie asked.

"In the church."

"Now who kissed you, baby?" my grandma wanted to know. "You said a man kissed you."

"Yeah. The priest."

Black preachers know God personally. Say, "You know, I first met God in 1929. Outside a little hotel in Baltimore. I was walking down the street, eating a tuna fish sandwich. In 1929, you ate anything you could get. And I heard this voice call unto me and the voice had power and majesty. And the voice said, 'Psst.' And I walked up to the voice and said, 'What?' And the voice got magnificent and holy and it resounded, 'Give me some of that sandwich.'"

I knew it was serious when everyone gasped after I identified the molester as a priest.

"What else, honey?"

"Well, Mama, after he kissed me, he said that he'd like to call me someday."

I saw my dad and Uncle Dickie past the point of being angry. Both held back laughter.

"And what'd you say?"

"I said, 'Call me tonight, later tonight,' and then I ran like hell," I said.

The next move was debated. My grandma and some aunties wanted to let it blow over, but my dad and uncle realized that they could probably get some money by blackmailing the priest. They hatched a plan. If the priest called, they told me to goad him into making incriminating comments. They'd listen on another extension. They also told me to arrange a meeting, at which they would surprise the priest and demand money.

"We'll collar him," my dad punned.

I was excited by the scam, but more so by suddenly being the center of attention. I also liked thinking about the monies my dad and uncle said we'd get. I thought that I might also get a cut and use it to go to the baseball games or the movies. Buy my way into the big time.

Later that night, the phone rang. My dad and uncle ran for the extensions. I nervously did my thing.

"Hi, baby," I purred in the soft, seductive voice they told me to use.

"Oh, my little doll," the priest said.

I heard the excitement in his voice. We cooed sweet nothings back and forth like that for a few minutes. I sensed my dad and uncle's scheme working. Suddenly my grandmother heard what was going on and called a halt to the charade from her bedroom.

"Don't do that to the boy!" she hollered.

Her loud, booming, angry voice threw me off the script and ended my lovey-dovey conversation with the priest before the crucial meeting was set. My dad and uncle scrambled into the kitchen. They made me promise to call him back. But then Grandma Marie yelled for us to get our ass into her bedroom and asked what the hell we were up to.

My father and Dickie denied everything. But I caved.

"Mama, I don't want to do this," I said.

Mama shook her head in disgust and ordered us to put an end to the scheming. It was disappointing. We had the priest hooked;

however, she wanted us to throw him back as if he was a small bass. Then she urged forgiveness.

"Richard," my grandmother said, "you've got to understand that everybody's human."

"Yes, Mama."

"Don't ever forget it," she continued. "No matter what they are. Everybody's human."

For a young black boy, that statement was hard to believe. It was clear that some people believed that they were more human than others. At my new school, Irving Elementary, I developed a crush on a little girl. She happened to be white. But she could've been any color, it didn't matter to me. I just liked her.

One day, as a token of my affection, I gave her a scratch board— the kind on which you scribble pictures and then lift up the plastic paper to erase the drawing. She promised to take it home and make it her favorite toy. I was pleased.

The next day her father showed up at school holding the toy. He looked mean. You weren't supposed to look at fourth-graders like that. He asked the teacher which "little nigger" had given his daughter the scratch pad. She pointed to me, and he ran straight up to me.

"Nigger, don't you ever give my daughter anything," he yelled.

That really put me back.

What the fuck had I done? Why was he calling me a nigger? Why did he hate me?

I mean I knew. I knew it was because I was black. But still, I didn't know why.

That shit is stuff that people like my grandmother warned me about. I also overheard others telling stories, nervously exchanging anecdotes, and such, but you don't believe it until you're actually confronted by it. Like a holdup or attack. You see it on the news every night, figuring it's always going to happen to someone else. Never you. But then some dude steps in your face and calls you a nigger.

If I was four and a half feet tall then, the girl's daddy cut six inches off. Zap. Six inches of self-esteem gone.

That was my indoctrination to the black experience in America. They don't teach that shit in school. But I'd learn, as every African American does to some degree, that such degradation and assault to one's dignity has gone on since the slave ships brought black people from Africa to this land of equality and opportunity.

I couldn't figure out why the teacher didn't defend me. She didn't say a word. My dad went to school the next day and confronted her. I'd never seen him so angry. I loved that he was defending me.

"How could you do that?" he asked. "How could you not say anything to that man?"

The teacher looked down. She shook her head, showing that she, too, was disgusted. At the man. At herself. My daddy gently patted her on the back. They reached some kind of understanding.

Then he turned to the little girl I'd tried to befriend.

"Did you get his present?" he asked.

"Yes," she sniffled. "But he wouldn't let me keep it."

"That's okay," I chimed in.

Or so I said.

But I didn't mean it.

My brain didn't segregate people by race. My eyes didn't see any one color. One of my favorite activities was going to the movies, where I lost myself in the fantasy projected on-screen. My heroes included

Tarzan, Rhonda Fleming, Milton Berle, Kirk Douglas, Sid Caesar, and Boris Karloff. I loved Jerry Lewis. I wanted to be John Wayne. I saw the *Red Ryder* cowboy serials over and over, and one time I went in the back to look for Robert Blake's Little Beaver character. I thought I'd be able to find him behind the screen. But the crew chased me out.

There were only a couple of theaters in Peoria that allowed black people inside. But then, having paid for tickets and popcorn the same as white people, we were restricted to sitting in the balcony. It was the same as public buses and washrooms. Except the odd thing was, nobody seemed to mind at the theater. They liked the balcony. The view was good, it was like a party, nobody threw shit on you.

But I wanted to sit up close, in the front row. You know how kids are? I wanted to feel as if I could jump into the screen.

However, one afternoon the manager grabbed my arm, yanked me from my chair, and told me I had to sit upstairs.

"In the 'Colored Section,'" he said. "Up where all you people are supposed to be."

"No, I ain't gonna do that," I said.

"Well, then you'll have to leave."

Niggers be holding their dicks. Some white people go, "Why you guys hold your things?"

Say, "You done took everything else, motherfucker."

I loved the movies, but the manager didn't give me a choice. I knew what was what.

So I left.

7

AT TWELVE YEARS OLD, I TRANSFERRED TO BLAINE SUMNER,
a primarily white school. By then, I'd given up on acquiring an
education. After all, I'd been raped, expelled, abused, and victimized
by the sting of racism. What more was there to learn?

*I couldn't lie to my old man because he could hypnotize me. He heard
my mind. Checked me right out.*

"Say, man, are you fucking up in school?" he asked.

Huh?

"Yes. I. Am."

In class, I let my motor idle. Between bells, I wondered if my
teachers were good fucks. Stuff like that.

I also jacked off.

*A lot of people didn't jack off. I used to jack off so much I knew pussy
couldn't be as good as my hand.*

My friend Andy and I had secret jack-off contests at our desks,
though one time in art class our X-rated antic wasn't as private as I

thought. After the bell, someone pointed out that all the desks had a front, except for mine. Everyone in class had watched.

"Ain't this a bitch," I said. "And here I thought I was being slick."

◆   ◆   ◆

I witnessed salvation come to people in a number of ways—drugs, gambling, women, and alcohol—and though I wouldn't say I was saved by Marguerite Yingst Parker, one of my teachers at Blaine, she did give me a shove in the right direction. Miss Parker was an attractive woman who had a pretty daughter about my age. I joked that I wanted to get together with her.

"Maybe we'll get married," I told my teacher. "Then you and I will be family."

"Oh, Richard," Miss Parker said sweetly.

What set Miss Parker apart from the rest was her ability to handle me. She did it with kindness and patience, a combination that's always slayed me. Ordinarily, I acted dumb in front of my teachers, but Miss Parker refused to believe my performances, no matter how convincing.

"I guess I'm too retarded for that," I whined.

Miss Parker always laughed at my silliness. Then she sat me down, assured me that I wasn't as dumb as I said, and in a gentle, sweet, reassuring voice she goaded me into at least trying to learn something.

In truth, she blackmailed me. If I would make an attempt at working, she said, then she would permit me to stand in front of the class each morning and tell jokes.

The deal was irresistible.

My routine was always something I'd picked up from a TV show. Red Skelton, Jerry Lewis, Sid Caesar. Sometimes I imitated friends;

other times I risked impressions of the school's teachers and bullies, who all of us knew were assholes. I never thought of myself as having a gift, but I made my classmates laugh, and when I heard their laughter, I felt good about myself, which was a pretty rare feeling. But nice. Real nice.

By high school, I'd tried running with gangs. But I was tough for about half a minute. That was it.

I was in every gang in Peoria. It had about five. I was in all of them. Whichever one was winning.

"That's my side!"

The real tough guys hung out at Proctor, a recreation center where they spent all day practicing how to be criminals. Fighting, rolling dice, drinking. Guys showed up at noon and hung around all day, waiting for the cops to come.

The scared pootbutts like me went to Carver Center, a safe haven thanks to the effort, vision, and devotion of Juliette Whittaker. A tiny young lady, she might've been the toughest soul in Peoria. She didn't take shit from anybody, and people who didn't even know her respected her for having something most others didn't—an education.

She was a black woman who came from good parents and had gone to college. That was something downright inspirational.

More so, instead of leaving for better neighborhoods that had higher-paying jobs, Miss Whittaker stayed in Peoria. She had beliefs about doing good, a conviction that she could help kids like me realize their dreams—if they dared to dream in the first place. She was good.

I picked up on that. Although Miss Whittaker reminded me of a toad, I saw the beauty inside her. Her smile made you forget about things. That's beauty. I proposed to her a couple of times, but I guess I was too young for her.

She'd just started at Carver when we met in 1951. She was in the midst of staging the play *Rumpelstiltskin* and had cast all the parts except a small role of a guy who goes onstage and sneezes. It wasn't a walk-on as much as it was a walk-off. But I got it and was thrilled, especially when she gave me a script to take home and learn, though there was nothing in it for me to memorize.

I learned all the parts anyway, and when the kid who played the king came down with the flu, Miss Whittaker turned to me. No one in the history of the theater was more prepared to move up than I was, though my performance was unique. I modeled my portrayal of the king after my Uncle Dickie and turned the fairy tale into a black comedy.

"Hey, baby," I said to the miller's daughter, "you keep on spinning that straw into gold for me and I'll get you a car. Something fine. Something for your mama. I'll make you my woman..."

Miss Whittaker noticed my talent, quick wit, ambition, and need—especially my need. She began centering skits and revues around me. I had no trouble being the center of attention and generating laughs. The spotlight suited me. In fact, I once pasted my name over Marlon Brando's on a photo of a movie marquee I cut out of the newspaper.

I spent all day making up shit. Practicing. It was like some kids stood on the corner and sang. I talked.

My father was one of those eleven o'clock men.

"Say, where you going? Nigger, you ain't asked nobody if you could go no place. What, you're a man now. Okay, then get a job. I don't give a fuck where you're going. Be home by eleven. You understand eleven, don't you,

nigger? You can tell time, can't you? Eleven o'clock, you bring your ass home. I don't mean down the street singing with them niggers, either... And bring me back a paper."

But nothing starts happening till eleven-thirty. Dudes be standing around. You ask, "What you waiting on, nigger?"

"Eleven-thirty. We gonna pitch a bitch at eleven-thirty."

I'd have to go home with my blue nuts.

"I thought I told you to be home at eleven," my dad yelled. "I don't want to hear that shit. I'm gonna kick your ass."

"Can I jack off first?"

Most of the shit I said was true. I just reported on what I saw and heard, adding a twist here and there.

"Your shoes are run over so much, looks like your ankles is broke."

Shit like that.

I did a character called the Rummage Sale Ranger. The Rummage Sale Ranger was a black superhero, but he was too poor to have his own shit. He had to go to the rummage sale. Find some woman's tights. Steal a fucking cape because he was out of change. Shoes that were too big. Nothing fit right.

Kids at the center loved the shit. The material flowed from my mouth without stopping, which was a problem for some.

Like Mr. Fink, my science teacher. But I gave him reason.

Mr. Fink was serious about teaching. I sat in the back row and entertained my neighbors as if I was at the Comedy Store working out a new routine. One day he got so fed up, he grabbed me by the scruff of the neck and took me downstairs. Just to show I had a sense of humor, I took a swing at him.

That was it.

He opened the front door to the school and literally threw my ass on the ground. Out of school.

"Don't come back," he said.

The door slammed shut with a loud bang. I knew there was no use arguing my way back inside. It was as if school was a train ride and the conductor was talking to me.

"Eighth grade. End of the line!"

"Aw, shit," I said out loud.

Then I thought about my folks. What were they going to say?

"Fuck," I said. "Now I got to go home and deal with those people."

8

EVERYBODY LISTENED TO WHAT HAPPENED. MY GRANDMOTHER.
My dad. Viola. My aunts and uncles. They then taught me the
lesson you learn after leaving school.

"It's okay," my dad said. "But I'll tell you this. If you don't put
nothing in the pot, you don't get nothing out."

Dinner that night was my last free meal. The next day I began
looking for a job.

As a fourteen-year-old high school dropout, I had low expectations. I begged local shop owners, and eventually I got a job cleaning
a strip club. Sweeping and mopping. My problem was that I liked
the show more than I did the work. The club's owner complained to
Uncle Dickie, who confronted me.

"He says the girls lay down on the stage and get all dirty," Dickie
explained to me. "What's the matter, boy?"

"I can do the sweeping," I said. "But I can't do no mopping. My
arms too skinny."

Next, I shined shoes at the Pierre Marquette Hotel. I enjoyed
that. I thought I was Numero Uno. I made the shine cloth crack like
a bullwhip. Told jokes. The money was easy and the conversation
good.

But I fell in with some bad guys who persuaded me there was an easier way to make money. By stealing it. One afternoon, we targeted a small grocery store in the neighborhood. As one guy went in and distracted the owner, another guy and I opened the cash register and grabbed the coins from the box. Nothing fancy. Plain old till-tapping. Except I dropped the coins. My friends ran. The owner calmly walked toward me, shaking his head in disgust.

"Boy, what the hell are you doing?" he yelled.

I froze and saw my future.

"We've got your son down here at headquarters. What about it?"

"Fuck him."

I'd be praying something would happen to him on the way down to the station. But he always showed up.

"I'm going to get you out, nigger. But then I'm gonna kick your ass."

My hands went straight up. There was nothing in them. I did one of those looks that said, "Who? Me?"

"Yes, nigger. I'm talking to you. Put that money back."

I put the coins back real nice, as if that would make it like nothing ever happened.

"I'm gonna tell your daddy," he threatened.

My so-called friends stood outside, looking through the window and laughing.

"And don't come back here no more," the owner added.

That hurt. Because that was my local store. I went there all the time.

About then Dickie was picked up for dope and went to jail. I remember when the cops got him: he was holding a big box of counterfeit money. Right before they cuffed him, he set it on top of a garbage can. Real calm. They never bothered to check it.

He went to prison in Michigan. He did about three years and came out a changed man.

He said to me, "Richard, I can only tell you one thing about prison."

"What's that?"

"Don't ever go."

I spent about half my pay at Yako's Liquor Store, where I ate pickled pig's feet, drank ice-cold beer, and bullshitted about the future. I didn't expect to stay employed at the packing company forever. Eventually, I figured on buying a pair of steel-toed shoes and punching a clock at the Caterpillar tractor company. Work, pension, die. In between, I'd get fucked up and watch TV and chase pussy.

Getting some pussy beats anything. I ain't lying. Coming is a lot of fun. I never got no pussy when I was a legal teenager. You had to sing to get pussy. Be one of those niggers on the corner who sang. I couldn't sing.

Besides, the girls weren't giving no pussy in the fifties. It was very seldom you got any parts of pussy. You'd be tongue kissing and your dick got harder than the times in '29. Nuts would go up into your stomach and you said, "Oh, baby, you gotta give me something now."

"I'm not giving anything," she said. "I'm on my period."

"You're on your period again? You gonna bleed to death, bitch."

At seventeen, I started fucking regularly. One was an attractive little package.

She and I used to hide out in the garage of a house my family owned on Goodwin. It wasn't the Playboy mansion, but it was kind of our private place.

It was pure fun.

I used to wrestle with her for two hours. That's when those rubber panties came out—those long rubber panties. And every time I'd get a grip, she'd move and I'd lose my grip and have to wrestle two more hours. And by the time I'd got them, I was too tired. "I'll see you tomorrow."

Then her father would catch us. There'd be a knock at the door. "What are you doing here, Mr. Pryor?"

"Oh, nothing. Just sitting here on the couch with my pants off."

I fell in love with that girl. Fell hard.

But then I loved falling in love.

Looking back, that turned out to be my curse. Falling in love, you know. It was never enough.

In late 1956, she took all the fun out of what we had going. She said she was pregnant.

For a moment, I thought the baby was mine. But she had slept with lots of people, including my dad. Nine months later she gave birth to a little girl. My Aunt Maxine reassured me that the baby wasn't mine.

This was revelatory, a weight off my back.

I was like, "Oh, somebody else claimed it?"

She said, "Yeah. I was out in the chicken shack and someone else said it was his baby."

Well, that was all the excuse I needed. The little girl grew up with her mother and grandmother in Peoria. I saw her occasionally, and eventually we got to know each other. Not an ideal relationship. Just a fact of life.

In 1958, I volunteered for the Army. I ask myself why I did something like that, a chickenshit like me.

I was serving my country. It was either that or six months.

I wanted out of Peoria. I wanted to see something different. No place in particular. Just beyond, you know.

I took the train to Chicago, went to the induction office, and spent the day taking tests. I must've done okay, because right after, I was sworn in. They gave me a free round-trip train ticket that got me home and back to Chicago.

To me, that was exciting shit.

Basic training was at Fort Leonard Wood, in Missouri. I received eight weeks of plumbing school.

Once again I was covered in shit.

I went to kill class. Turned me around. I thought the Army was like hunting, camping, a little fishing. But I learned to kill from a guy who killed in World War Two, and then they couldn't stop him. So they gave him a job.

"Can't let him on the streets, so we'll let him train these guys for World War Three."

Then my papers come in, and I was transferred to Idar-Oberstein in Germany. For an eighteen-year-old who'd never been farther than Springfield or Bloomington, it was exciting. Idar-Oberstein sounded like an exotic woman.

Then reality. I called my sergeant and told him I was on my way to the base.

"I'm so happy you're coming," he said.

"Thank you, sir," I said.

"Yeah," he laughed. "I've been working with a nigger for the last three years."

Uh-oh, I thought.

"Yes, sir," I said. "Well, I'm glad I'm here too, sir. Yes, sir."

I expected Germany to be a little freer, but the *Fräuleins* were skinny rather than fat, and when I ventured to the section where all the bars were located, I found that out of like 150 bars only three let in blacks. Why should you have been surprised, Rich? Well, I was, because I thought all that shit was behind me.

Unfortunately, I met a woman whose boyfriend was a bartender in one of the white bars, and one night I went there. Her boyfriend, who usually called the MPs on me, wasn't working that night, so I had a chance. But before I ordered my first beer, a fight broke out between two U.S. soldiers, and before I knew it, I heard someone cry out, "Nigger!"

I glanced around. There was no one else of any color there but me. I ran upstairs, where the strippers changed clothes, begging the first girl I saw to help. She gave me a look of hate that I knew too well from back home.

"Get out of here," she said in a heavily accented voice.

"You don't understand. They're fighting down there."

"Get out of here. I call police."

The MPs arrived at the same time I snuck outside and ran back to the barracks. I never forgot that stripper, though.

Of course, you never forget the cruel ones.

But there were other, kinder women, thank God.

My kind of women. The kind who liked to fuck. This one woman let me give her head, which was a revelation, something that changed my life, because until then, my family only fucked in one position—up and down.

My uncle had said, "Boy, don't you ever kiss no pussy. I mean that. Whatever you do in life, don't kiss no pussy."

I couldn't wait to kiss the pussy. He'd been wrong about everything else. Women had to beat me off.

"It's enough! It's enough. Two days!"

Eventually the Army turned me into a vicious killing machine. The transformation occurred in full one weekend night as our unit watched the movie *Imitation of Life*. This white soldier laughed at the wrong spots. Several of us finally took exception, including a big black soldier, who got into a slugfest with the white guy.

But my guy was a dumb motherfucker in terms of fighting. The white boy seriously hurt my guy's ass.

A crowd gathered. People wanted blood. We'd spent months training for combat, but this turned into the biggest battle anyone had come close to, and I knew my guy was going down if something didn't happen.

From within the crowd of soldiers, I reached into my pocket and drew out a switchblade. Pushed the button.

Flifft!

No one but me suspected anything. I waited for the right moment. Then I stabbed the white motherfucker in the back six or seven times. He didn't stop, though. You know? He kept throwing punches. As soon as I realized he wasn't going down, I ran in the opposite direction, tossing the knife into the bushes on my way to the barracks.

A while later, the white dude came in accompanied by an angry-looking MP. I peeked at the white guy's back. His T-shirt was shredded from my stabbing, and soaked with blood. I thought, Goddamn, I did that and he didn't even stop. Didn't even feel it. Why didn't he feel it?

He stared at me like that bull from the packing plant where I'd worked. Then he tore off his shirt.

"See what you did to me, chickenshit?" he said.

"Wasn't me."

He said, "Yes, it was. You're the one. See all these holes? You're the asshole nigger who did this."

"No, I didn't do it."

My denials meant shit. An MP threw my ass in jail. There wasn't anything in that cell except for me, the cement floor, and a single, annoying light bulb. I fell onto the cot and began to think seriously about getting the fuck out of jail and the Army.

The base commander agreed. He was on the verge of retirement, and the last thing he wanted to deal with was a silly enlisted man fucking up regulations.

I was lucky. Lucky I didn't kill that white guy and luckier still that they didn't kill me.

Because back then, the way things were, few people outside of Peoria would've missed one more dead black man.

9

I RETURNED TO PEORIA SPEAKING ENOUGH BROKEN GERMAN TO impress the local girls, but I was disappointed that I hadn't connected with the service. I had hoped to start a new career, something with more future and security than working at the packing plant or Caterpillar.

Instead, I settled into the most popular career path among young uneducated black men—unemployment.

I allowed plenty of free time for inspiration to find me.

I remember seeing Redd Foxx and Dick Gregory on television and thinking that I could do something similar. I had no trouble making people laugh. I made a fool out of myself as good as the next guy. Did it all the time. The guys I hung out with said I was a funny motherfucker. Shit, I might as well get paid for it.

I knew where to go, and one day I walked into Harold's Club and asked Harold Parker, the club's owner, for work. Harold's was a black and tan club, meaning both whites and blacks went there. Harold himself was like that. We used to say he was too light to be bright.

"What do you do?" he asked.

"I sing and play piano."

Okay, I lied. I didn't do either. But Harold was a friend of my father's.

"How much you expecting to make?" he asked.

I answered, "Not much."

"That's good," he said. "'Cuz you won't."

For my nightclub debut, I sat at the piano and improvised using the three or four chords I knew. I sang whatever words popped into my head. I saw that people didn't know whether I was putting them on or weird. But I put in enough time for the waitresses to serve their drinks and collect their tips.

Afterward, I tried to look cool, but when Harold came up to me backstage, I still had sweat pouring off me.

"You've got more nerve than anybody I've ever seen," he said. "Would you like to keep coming?"

"Yes, sir," I said. "I would like to do that."

Harold also hired Sonny Stinson, a real singer, who brought his own band. He was the main attraction. I did my thing during their breaks. After a while, I realized that the audience responded better to my jokes than to my singing and so, shit, I wasn't stupid. Talking was easier than making up songs. I told jokes, did impressions of Dean Martin, Jerry Lewis, and Sammy Davis, Jr., and sometimes I simply picked up a book or the newspaper and read the shit in a strange voice while adding funny asides.

One of my earliest bits was a takeoff on "Person to Person," the TV show, on which host Edward R. Murrow interviewed famous people in their homes. In my act, I wondered what might happen if instead of talking to a celebrity, Murrow walked in on a dirt-poor black family in Mississippi.

"Hi, Mistah Murrah. Just step over the chickens. Yes, that's it. We're going to have one for dinner if you want to stay.

"Yes, sir, that's our chair. And our TV. And our sofa. The wall-paper is newspaper. Put it up ourselves.

"That house in the back?

"No, that ain't no guest house. We piss in there. Go ahead, if you need to. We'll keep the chickens back."

◆　　　◆　　　◆

I was desperate to matter. I wanted to grow and bloom like the patch of sunflowers I admired as a boy. The laughter and attention I got on stage fed that desire.

Then I received an additional boost. Sonny Stinson introduced me to marijuana and uppers. I'd never tried either. I drank, but drugs were new to me.

"It's part of show business," said Sonny.

Whether or not that was true didn't matter once I tried the shit. I liked the buzz. It eased my pain and insecurity, erased the fear, turned me into a whole new man. Sometimes I stayed up two or three days straight, feeling so cool and jive. Eventually, Sonny tired of me always asking for freebies.

"You want more, it's gonna cost you," he said.

Shit, I didn't care. I loved the high, hated the crash. Said I'll take two instead. Stayed awake forever. Then at two in the morning on the second or third day of being awake, I'd be screaming for help.

"Please, God, there's an Indian playing a drum inside me. Tell him to stop."

"That's your heart."

"Well, tell it to stop. Let me sleep."

"HA-HA-HA!"

I was as easily hooked on women, too. My next love, Patricia, was a nice, tender little thing, who reminded me of the Patricia Neal character in the movie *Hud*. Same name, same situation. She probably shouldn't have gotten involved with a confused young comedian who didn't have a plan. But, hey, I made about $50 a week and I thought that was good, you know?

For us, it was.

But in 1960 I didn't know certain stuff. Patricia got pregnant. I felt responsible, which might've been the first and last time I did. But my dad told me flat out I didn't have to marry her.

"You don't have to do this, son," he said.

Yes, I did. Just to spite him I did.

Geez, I was a sick puppy.

Patricia and I married in the little corner house on Goodwin. My grandmother, dad, and Viola were among those who attended the event. They came when Richard Jr. was born, too. At the hospital, I stared at him for the longest time. He looked like a little ape, and when I told my dad that, he laughed.

"So did you," he said. "Like a little gorilla. That's what Mama said about you."

"Yeah?" I muttered. "Then I guess he's mine."

But that was about all. After Richard Jr. was born, Pat and I quit living together.

Why'd I split?

Because I could.

10

BY 1962, I ALSO STARTED PERFORMING AT COLLINS' CORNER, another black and tan nightclub, though it was actually more black than tan. The club's owner, Bris Collins, promoted me from opening act to emcee, which paid between $70 and $10 a week and gave me an excuse to hang out with the headliner, a pretty girl from St. Louis who could sing her ass off.

She had a big act that included dancers and backup singers, most of whom, I discovered, were transvestites. Men dressing up as girls. I was greatly relieved to find a few real females. One sang, one danced, and one had a sister who looked more like a brother. I always thought she was a man. Then one night she gave me some pussy. I swear I thought she was going to pull out some kind of dick.

But she didn't. She liked me.

I listened to them tell stories of playing the different black-owned clubs in the Midwest that formed the Blackbelt circuit and dreamed of hitting the road just as they did. It was my way out.

"Maybe one day I'll emcee a rock 'n' roll show," I said to Bris Collins.

That day came sooner than I imagined.

One day my woman—this whore who'd been given to me by my dad—told me to beat her. I didn't know what she was talking about, but she screamed, "Hit me. Hit me." Well, I didn't know that when a woman told you to hit her you weren't supposed to go crazy. But I went crazy. I started fighting as if it was a real fight. Bruised and hurt, she ran to my father. It looked as if he might beat me.

"What the fuck are you doing?" he yelled. "You don't know how to beat a whore."

"But she said to hit her," I explained.

"Get out of here," he said.

"What?" I asked, realizing he was serious about kicking me out of the house. "What'd you say?"

"Get your ass outta here!"

I hadn't planned on such a hasty departure, but I had no choice. I grabbed some clothes, some cash, and a little alto saxophone, which I later pawned to buy groceries, and walked in a swirl of confusion over to Collins' Corner. I didn't know what I was going to do or where I was going to go, only that I wasn't going to stick around Peoria, and as I slammed the door behind me, I said, "You'll see, motherfucker. Someday, you'll see."

At Collins' Corner, I told both the guys who were girls and the real girls what had happened. They invited me to travel with them to East St. Louis, where they were booked into the Faust Club, a club on the Blackbelt circuit. I couldn't believe my luck. One minute kicked out of the house, no prospects. The next I was on the road in show business.

I was too raw for the Faust Club, whose acts were all experienced. But the club's emcee watched me work a few times and tried to help. My routines weren't bad, he said, but my delivery was.

"You've got to talk to the people," he said. "You always look like you want to kill them. Persuade 'em."

"Okay."

When my friends moved on, I was left to fend for myself. But I had picked up on how the system worked from other performers, particularly from one dancer. She had given me the mystery eye and led me into her dressing room. I mentioned that I'd been in the Army, in Germany. She was impressed and asked what I'd done there.

"I learned to eat pussy," I said.

Smiling, she eased back on the tattered dressing-room sofa and told me that if I ate her pussy, she'd speak to the club owner at her next job and get me hired as the emcee. And that was how things operated. You worked a little on stage and a little off it. I also realized why they called the Army "the service."

On the Blackbelt, there were no booking agents or managers who got you jobs. Instead, the performers traded information among themselves—strippers, musicians, dancers. They told the club owners who was good, bad and indifferent, who liked to drink, fight, gamble, do drugs, and shit like that.

There weren't a lot of options, so basically you went wherever you were wanted and hoped it worked out.

Towns flew by in a blur. Cleveland, Chicago, Buffalo, and so on. I took cars, buses, trains, hitchhiked. It was hard times, but exciting times. I was going someplace else. Every day was different, a surprise, an adventure through uncharted territory, and it forced me to sharpen my skills and learn my craft just as Redd Foxx, Dick Gregory, Godfrey Cambridge, and other black comics had done before me.

It was like going to school, especially this one funky club in Youngstown, Ohio. That's where I discovered God blessed me to be stupid enough not to know better. Everybody, it seemed, but me knew the place was owned by shady characters. Tough guys. People who settled arguments by throwing guys off bridges and such.

For real.

None of these stories bothered Satin Doll, the beautiful singer who headlined the club. Then toward the end of our run, I heard her crying in her dressing room. I walked in and asked what was wrong. I expected to hear that her lover had been fitted with concrete shoes. It was worse.

"They aren't going to pay us," she sobbed.

"Not going to pay who?" I asked. "Motherfuckers aren't going to pay me? I was raised better than that shit."

Back then, I carried a blank pistol with me. For protection, of course. Shows how ignorant I was.

So I got the gun, busted into the club's office, and ordered the motherfuckers to give me the money they owed me.

I talked my best black shit. That usually scared the average white motherfucker. But you know how it is when you do something and the motherfucker don't react and you can feel there's something wrong?—and you got the gun!

You think there's something wrong. There's some look missing in this motherfucker's face.

I'm sure those men are there today, laughing. Because he just started laughing.

"This fucking kid," he said. "Ah-ha-ha-ha-ha."

Then he called his partner, Tony.

"Hey, do it again, Rich. Put the gun away and do it again. Say 'Stick 'em up.' Ha-ha-ha-ha! You fucking kid. I like you. Fucking stick 'em up. Hey, Tony, was you scared? Ha-ha-ha…"

It got worse in Pittsburgh, where I met a singer. She liked me a lot. Why, I don't know. But it was nice. Except I didn't know enough to keep my mouth shut.

Thinking I was a big shot, I told people we were going out and that she was giving me money and shit. Someone told her and she came looking for me, seeking revenge. At the confrontation, backstage, I thought she was going to do serious damage to me, so I beat her ass first. I didn't think about hitting a woman as much as I thought about my own survival.

But shit.

Pittsburgh was like a small town. Her father knew some cops, and one night, as I was about to go to sleep, they busted in the rooming house where I lived, fixing to turn me inside out. Once they saw me, though, all 150 pounds of skin and bones and no muscle, they must've felt as if she should've taken me, or that at least it was a fair fight.

Instead of beating me up, they let me get dressed and we shot shit as they took me to jail.

Still, it wasn't a good situation. Skinny black kid. Broke. In jail. My lawyer told me to keep quiet in court.

I tried, but...

"Ninety days," the judge said.

Shit.

I remembered what Uncle Dickie had said about going to jail, which was don't. I also remembered that Spinks, the player from Peoria who'd helped me lose my virginity, had always sworn he wasn't going to ever go to jail, and when they finally sent him off, he stayed true to his word by dropping dead of a heart attack as soon as he heard the clink of his cell door being shut.

But it wasn't so bad. In jail, I met a guy on his way out who knew my Aunt Maxine. Through him, I got her to send me twenty bucks, which I used to play the numbers. I put a dime on 313 and it came up. I won $70 and after doing thirty-five days, I used my winnings to buy myself out of the pokey.

It was freezing the day I got out of jail. On my way back to the club, I heard Sammy Davis, Jr., had performed the night before and was still in town. For some reason, I decided that I had to meet Sammy, who would become a friend years later, so I walked to his hotel, found out his room, and sat in a chair at the end of the hall. Just sat there.

For hours, nothing happened. Every now and then, a policeman shuffled through and gave me the once-over, but in my suit I appeared to be part of Sammy's entourage. Or at least someone who had reason to be there.

A few times, Sammy peeked out his door and saw me. Once, one of his guys brought me a plate of food, which I devoured. He probably figured I was some bum hoping for a handout, but in all honesty I think I just wanted to shake his hand and hope some luck rubbed off on me.

The next day, Sammy finally came out of the room. I stood up, grinned like a fool with nothing to say.

But it was Sammy Davis, Jr.!

"What's happening?" he said.

"Well, I was working in town," I stammered, "And I thought I'd see you and maybe get a job with you or something."

Sammy nodded. He let me bum a cigarette and gave me a bit of hope. But he was so jive. He had the walk, the talk, the attitude. Didn't mind being a star one bit. It was a beautiful thing to see. Made me envious.

From there, I went to Buffalo, where I met Donnie Simpson, a struggling comic like myself, though he talked more shit than anybody I knew, including me. He dragged me to Windsor, Canada, and then to Toronto, always promising we'd meet more beautiful women and earn bigger paychecks. Finally, up in Toronto, we ran out of clubs.

It was 1963. I remember opening a copy of *Newsweek* magazine and seeing an article on Bill Cosby. It devastated me. I told Donnie, and later reiterated to others, "Goddamn it, this nigger's doing what I'm fixing to do. I want to be the only nigger. Ain't no room for two niggers."

"Then why's your ass here, Rich?" he said. "You got to go to New York. That's where all them bit cats are."

11

I LOOKED AS GOOD AS COULD BE WHEN I ARRIVED IN NEW YORK. I wore a ragamuffin suit, a pencil-thin tie, and patent leather shoes. Although I had only $10 in my pocket, I looked like $50.

At the train station, I paid 50 cents to shower, slapped on some Canoe cologne, walked outside and breathed in Manhattan. Skyscrapers, taxis, crowds racing along the sidewalks. It was a lot to take in for someone with no place to go. I heard alarms go off in my head and wondered what the hell I'd done.

The only place I knew in Manhattan was the Apollo Theater, in Harlem. I caught a bus uptown, got off at 125th Street, and wandered around. I didn't know a soul, but seeing all those black people made me feel better.

At the Apollo, I met the guy who was in charge of booking acts. He looked and sounded like someone who'd seen and heard everything and was just waiting till sometime later.

"I'd like to work here," I said. "I'm a comedian."

"Yes, right," he answered. "Why don't you try down at the Village."

This was my first time in New York, and perhaps I was dumber than dog shit, but wasn't this a city? A big city?

Why was he talking about a village?

He gestured.

"Downtown," he said.

I caught a bus and sat down next to a guy who listened to me ramble about how I'd come to town to be a comedian and didn't know anyone. I told him I planned to stay at the YMCA nearest the clubs and asked if he knew where that was. He insisted that I stay with him at his rooming house on Thirty-sixth Street.

The guy was gay, which scared me, but he turned out to be nice and helpful. He introduced me to the landlady, got me a room, and then gave me a talk on who was naughty and nice in the area.

In 1963, the Village was alive. Full of cats similar to me. A bunch of hobos looking for work. I met talented young comics like J. J. Barry, Martin Harvey Freeberg, and Ron Carey. They educated me about the club scene. Someone told me to introduce myself to Manny Roth, the owner of Café Wha?, and before long, I was opening for Superman Victor Brady and his Trinidadian steel band, telling jokes such as:

"I watch a lot of television, and so I see those commercials, like the one where the woman says, 'Honey, I got a giant in my washer.'

"And her husband says, 'Yea, well he better be gone before I get home.'"

Once I decided I was going to be in New York for a while, I took a small apartment on Fourteenth Street. It was a strange place. You could lock the door, but any key opened it. One night a thief broke in just after I'd gone to bed. I heard the door open. Then somebody walked in. He began rummaging through my stuff when he felt the burn of my gaze like a flashlight beam and turned around.

"Um, I think you've got the wrong room," I said calmly.

The dude played it just as cool and said, "I guess you're right," and then left.

He wasn't the only strange character I met. No, not in New York.

Once, I was in a restaurant with a group of people, including a beautiful lady who flirted with me. She was white, and her advances really upset the guy next to me. As soon as I picked up on this, I added grease to the frying pan, suggesting that she change seats so she could sit beside me. A few minutes later, we left for a nearby hotel.

But then the joke turned on me. As we sat on the bed in the hotel room, I put my arm around her and started rubbing her sumptuous body. We worked up to that magic point, and just as I was about to ask her to give me head, my hand touched her arm. It was like no other arm that I'd ever felt.

In fact, it was wooden. I checked it out with my fingernail. Hard as a tree. Could've used the motherfucker for kindling. Right away, my dick said adios, retreating into my stomach, and I guess she sensed my discovery.

"Does that bother you?" she asked.

"No," I squeaked. "But it scares the hell out of my dick."

Before long, I became a regular at the Bitter End, the Living Room, Papa Hud's, and all the other clubs. The scene reminded me of Harold's and Collins' Corner back in Peoria, but instead of Sonny Stinson, the performers were Bob Dylan, Richie Havens, and Bill Cosby. I met George Carlin at the Café Au Go Go and introduced myself to Woody Allen at the Bitter End. Woody said: "Stick around, watch me, and you'll learn something."

But oddly, I learned more from a hooker in Baltimore. I was working the Playboy Club when I met her, and after the show she took me to her place and said, "I want you to hear something." Then she put on a green-colored record album, something that I'd never seen.

"What's this?" I asked.

"Listen," she said.

Then I heard Lenny Bruce for the first time.

"Lima, Ohio."

I'd never heard anything like him before, especially his bit about the kid who went to the hobby shop to buy some airplane glue but was afraid to ask for it. Instead, he asked for everything else, all sorts of crap, one item after another. Finally, after he'd gotten everything else, he blurted out that he also wanted something like two thousand tubes of glue.

That destroyed me. I went fucking crazy.

One night at the Wha? I got offstage just as a guy ran in all excited because Lenny Bruce was outside taking pictures. Lenny! My God. I raced outside to see the brightest and bravest of all.

Outside, I saw a crowd gathered around a mounted policeman and his horse—this big brown thing that had crapped in the street —and through the mass of laughing people, I spotted Lenny. Scuttling about, he held a camera and, as near as I could tell, was snapping pictures of the horse's dick.

That was strange, you know. Unfortunately, that's as close as I ever came to seeing him perform.

Bill Cosby was the guy who was most envied. I remember seeing a picture of Bill on the cover of *Time* magazine. Every comedian I knew had seen it and was jealous as an ugly whore. But damn, Bill was good. Once when I played the Wha?, I heard Bill was at the Cellar, and so between sets I went over to see his work for myself.

"Noah?"

"Who's that?"

"God."

"Yeah, right."

The man was amazing. Truly amazing. Do you hear me? I was amazed.

On my way back to the Wha?, I decided that's who I was going to be from then on.

Bill Cosby.

Richard Cosby.

I grabbed the crook. It was the wrong move. He threw me down. I got up again. He knocked me down. I got up. He kicked me down. I got up. He said, "Get up."

I said, "Ha, haaaaa!"

Then my wife threw him across the furniture. She slapped me. The police came. She beat them up. They took her away.

Me and the crook livin' happily ever after.

If the material wasn't exactly Bill's, the delivery was. So much so that I should've informed people.

But the other comics caught on and asked, "What the fuck happened?"

I said, "I'm going for the bucks."

I finally met Bill Cosby at Papa Hud's. There was no doubt in anyone's mind, he was on his way. Like a fucking rocket ship, Cosby was going to the top. You could've put every dollar you had on that number. But he was still nice to me. He advised me to "find my own thing." Then one day I told Bill that I was booked at the Apollo, my first big show there.

"I'm opening for Billy Eckstine," I said. "My name's even on the marquee."

I convinced Bill to jump in a cab and go uptown with me so I could show him my name on the Apollo's marquee. On the way, he told me to be careful. Not to cuss. Not to talk foul. Not to act no fool.

"But I'm being paid to be a fool," I said.

"You know what I mean," he replied.

At West 125th Street, the cab pulled up in front of the legendary theater. Bill and I got out and stared at the marquee.

BILLY ECKSTINE

AND

OPENING ACTS

Bill scratched his head and looked at me, puzzled.

"Where's your name, Rich?" he asked. "I see Billy Eckstine's. But not yours."

"Right there," I said, pointing. "Underneath."

"I don't see it."

"What do you mean? Right there. 'Opening Acts.'"

"That isn't your name."

"But it's me," I insisted. "I'm one of the opening acts."

On August 31, 1964, I made my TV debut on Rudy Vallee's summer variety show, "On Broadway Tonight." Rudy himself, over the producer's objections, insisted on putting me on the show. I considered it a stroke of luck, my first opportunity at nationwide exposure. Back then, Cosby, Dick Gregory, and Nipsey Russell were among the few black comics who appeared on TV. I was happy to join them.

Nervous and stiff as I stared into the camera, I began my set with an introduction.

"I'm gonna tell you folks a few things about myself, because a lot of you probably don't know me," I said.

"I'm not a New Yorker. My home is Peoria, Illinois. I had a wild neighborhood, I gotta tell you. Because my mother's Puerto Rican, my father's a Negro, and we lived in a big Jewish tenement building —in an Italian neighborhood.

"So every time I went outside, they'd yell, 'Get him! He's all of them!' "

I continued:

"When I was young I used to think my people didn't like me. Because they used to send me to the store for bread and then they'd move."

After the show, my family called to congratulate me. My dad, in particular, was tickled.

He said, "We're proud of you, son. At least you aren't sticking nobody up."

12

BY THE MID-1960s, MY REPUTATION AS A COMIC HAD SPREAD beyond the downtown nightclubs, where I was as well known for acting strange as I was for getting laughs. Thanks to appearances on television variety shows like "Merv Griffin" and the "Kraft Music Hall," I entered the mainstream.

My personal life remained less conventional. I caught women as if they were taxis. But you know how sometimes you'll get a driver who's strange? That happened to me when I became involved with Tia Maria, a prostitute.

She took me back to her apartment. Introduced me to cocaine. Her friend, the white lady.

"Come on, everybody's doing it," she said.

"Okay. I'll try some."

I started snorting little tiny pinches, saying, "I know I ain't gonna get hooked. Not on coke. My friends have been snorting fifteen years and they aren't hooked.

She set out nice little piles the size of small pearls. Real pretty. And I liked it.

Yes, I did. From the first snort. It made me feel cool. Got me brave.

I started snorting little teeny things. Didn't even make any noise. Coke etiquette, Jack. "Pass the album, please. Oh, no more for me." Six months later. Oink. Snarf. Licking the album. Trying to get a freeze.

Tia Maria was nice—for a liar. We would be laying in bed and she'd suddenly announce that I had to leave. Immediately.

"Why, baby?"

"My uncle is coming over. I don't want him to know you're here."

She never wanted me to meet him, and for some reason I never asked why. I'd do as she say.

I got dressed and left. Then I pleaded to come back. Wanted the pussy.

"Oh, God, are you calling again? God, Richard, please, don't do this to yourself. I mean, why don't you go home and bathe or something."

Then I heard her on the phone. Say, "Just a minute, John."

One night Tia Maria had a big party at her house. Everybody got smashed on something. I asked where she got a piece of furniture that I admired. She said it was a present from her uncle. Someone else asked his name. One of her girlfriends heard the question and chimed in, "It came from John."

"John?" I asked.

"You know, John," she said with a wink.

Everyone laughed. Finally, I got the joke. Tia Maria had a sugar daddy. Her uncle.

"You're a whore?"

"I'm whatever you want me to be, baby."

Tia Maria turned into a wild, crazy creature when she got high. She liked to take off all her clothes, climb out the apartment window and walk onto the ledge of her building. With her titties blowing in the wind, she yelled at people on the street. Put on one of the most exciting shows in town.

Part of me enjoyed watching.

You think up some weird sexual fantasies when you be on coke. You say shit like, "Baby, I got a great idea. I want you to get up on the roof. I'm gonna run around the house three times. On the third time I want you to jump off on my face."

Part of me also hated it. Maybe she got off on that shit, but it scared the hell out of me. I yelled for her to get back inside, come to her senses—like I had any myself.

"Leave the bitch alone," a friend of mine said.

"But she's going to jump," I said. "One of these days she's going to jump."

"So? That's her business."

After several more of those episodes, I knew our days were numbered. I couldn't take that much excitement. There were other womens around, including Sonya, a friend of Tia's, who was a beautiful girl. I fucked her a few times, and then I got the guilties so bad that I confessed to Tia.

She freaked out. I thought she might throw me off the damned balcony. But not because of the obvious. See, Sonya was Tia's lady. They were lesbians. I didn't know until then, and once it was in the open my ass was the one shoved out the door.

Then I met Maxine Silverman. She dated my friend Frank. One night I got a girl and the four of us went out on a double date. By the end of the evening, I liked Maxine better than my date. I spent the next couple days charming my way into her life.

Maxine was a phenomenal chick, the cutest white girl I'd ever seen. She zoomed along the fast lane. She knew things, sophisticated things that I'd never learned, like which forks to use at a nice restaurant and shit like that, and she grooved right along with me in treating life like a party.

Somebody told me if you put coke on your dick you could fuck all night. Shouldn't have told me. My dick had a Jones. Six hundred dollars a day just to get my dick hard.

We were kids. If Maxine and I had really gotten to know each other, we would've discovered we were mismatched. We had fun together, but we didn't belong as a couple. It didn't stop me from putting her on a pedestal. That's what I did with women. Raised them high. Treated them like royalty. Until I got them up high. Once that was accomplished, I didn't care anymore, you know?

But what do you say?

Nothing. You just feel bad. Let that weirdness gnaw at you like termites.

"Hey, Rich, what's wrong?" my conscience asked.

"Nothing."

"I know you're lying. You can tell me."

"Fuck you."

The trouble starts when that shit visits you. One night after several days of nonstop snorting and drinking and snorting, I succumbed to a paranoid flittamajitter. My whole life dropped in uninvited.

Broke into my room like thugs collecting money. I didn't know what the hell was happening, but it scared the fuck out of me, no doubt about that.

Locked in my bedroom, I saw myself being stalked by people who wanted to kill me. Family members. Guys I knew. Dealers. Women I'd fucked and promised shit to. The womens wanted me dead most of all.

I kept checking the locks on my apartment door. I had about twelve of them. I kept turning them. Click-click. I was so fucked up that I missed a booking on "The Ed Sullivan Show." My agent called the next day as I was finally returning to normal and asked what happened.

"I have no idea," I said. "I'm just lucky to be here, you know?"

"I'll smooth it over, Rich," he said. "But listen: In this business, people talk. Don't blow it."

I made the next "Ed Sullivan Show." Got paid something like $500, which was a lot of money then. Maxine and I walked down Fifth Avenue feeling like we owned the world. We met up with musicians Dion and Kenny Rankin. In the Village, we bought some LSD. What did I know about acid? The guy who sold it to me said it was a cool high.

White dude gave me some shit. Talking 'bout how I'm gonna be trippin'. Shit, I ain't going no place without my luggage.

Neither Maxine nor I had tried LSD before, so we didn't know what to expect. We started out at a rock show, but by the time that shit kicked in we had made it back to the safety of our home. Thank God.

I can't imagine what it would've been like had we stayed out, because once I started tripping, I got into a thing with our kitty. Ordinarily, me and the cat didn't have much to do with each other. We put up with each other.

"Hi, Kitty. How ya doin'?"

"Don't talk to me, asshole. I see how you treat women."

Suddenly this cat follows me around as if we were attached, as if the cat was my shadow. Real close. Too close. Particularly for somebody on LSD. Wherever I went the cat crept right beside me, rubbing, touching, meowing. I thought the cat was fucking with me, you know?

"Get the fuck away."

"Fuck you, Rich."

I swear me and that cat got into an argument.

Hey, man, look at this. I can catch my hand.
Waaaaaaaaaaaaaa!

At one point, Maxine and I achieved a meeting of the minds, a perfect intersection of thought and awareness, something that happens only during an acid trip. Laughing hysterically, we stared deep into each other and shared a simultaneous thought: Our relationship was wrong. Then we laughed some more, and I said, "This ain't right, is it?" We should've quit right then. But we didn't.

Ohhhhhhhhhh, shiiiiiiiit.
I've got to get the fuck outta here.
Waaaaaaaaaaaaaaaaa!

It's amazing we survived the shit that happened. One day I gave our last $200 to some actor who wanted to fly to L.A. to audition for a movie. Over Maxine's objections, I wrote him a check. Late that night he broke into our apartment and stormed into the bedroom holding the check.

"Rich, they couldn't read your signature at the bank. You have to write me another one."

"I don't have to do anything now," I said. "I'm sleeping."

"Rich, please, man."

"Ask Maxine."

He woke her up. She got pissed all over again. She stormed out of the bedroom. I got angry at her for getting angry while this actor was angry at both of us for fucking up his big chance. Maxine ran onto the balcony and started screaming shit. Shakes of Tia Maria. Very high drama.

I said, "Max, take it easy."

We fought like truly mad people. We didn't even know what we were fighting about. We just fought."

Then she picked up a knife.

"I'm gonna cut you, motherfucker," she screamed.

"Go ahead, bitch."

You might say shit like that, but if you thought about it for a second, you'd know you don't mean it.

She kind of lunged. I kind of danced into the blade with my left arm. There was a slight collision. But the knife was extremely sharp. Sharp enough to cut through flesh with only the mildest of swipes.

I saw red.

Blood.

My blood!

I can't breathe. I don't remember how to breathe. Something's wrong.
I'm gonna die. I don't even know where the fuck I am. Shit. I'm gonna
die. I'm gonna die...

I rushed to the emergency room, where the admissions nurse gave me one of those ho-hum looks, handed me a clipboard with forms attached, and asked me to sit down and fill them out.

"With what? Blood? Look at my arm!"

"Here, use a pen."

Finally, someone recognized me from TV and took care of me. I got a shot of something that numbed my arm. Then a doctor stitched me up. As he sewed, he asked me how I'd gotten the gash.

"I was trying out a knife trick," I said.

"And so you stabbed yourself in the upper part of your arm?" he asked, not buying my explanation.

"Yeah. I don't have it down yet."

"Well, don't try it anymore. Please. For your own sake."

"Okay, Doc, I won't."

I lived the kind of drama and tragedy that made for great comedy, but I let only bits and pieces creep into my act. Instinct told me to do more, except the pressure was to go with the flow.

"Don't offend, Rich."

It was a politically charged time. Martin Luther King fought for equality and dignity. Malcolm clamored. But in terms of entertainment white America wanted its black comedians colorless.

Negro.

Colored.

Those were okay.

But as comedy writer Murray Roman, a nice man who didn't know any better than to reflect prevailing opinion, advised me, "Now I'd introduce Bill to my mother. But a guy like you...Don't mention the fact that you're a nigger. Don't go into such bad taste."

Don't say...

You can fuck white women and if they don't come, they say, "It's all right. I'll just lay here for a while and use a vibrator."

Black women, they'll talk about you. "Nigger, well, is that it? Hell, you got to grind my pussy. Oh, nigger, fuck me. Shit. Don't put my legs down, motherfucker."

The trouble was, I didn't know any better than to listen to Murray Roman and people like that. I didn't have a view of the big picture. I didn't know myself well enough. Charlie Chaplin had the Little Tramp, but I hadn't yet discovered my character, and that was because I tried so hard to be someone else. I didn't think about artistry as much as I did making monies.

Monies. That was the goal, the dream. The more the better. I figured the more distance I put between me and poverty, the happier I'd be.

Just tell jokes, Rich.

Tell stories.

Tell 'em like Bill would.

And so my routine included harmless spoofs of life in the ghetto such as when I pretended to be a doofus saying, "I heard a knock on the door. I said to my wife, 'There's a knock on the door.' And my wife said, 'That's peculiar. We ain't got no door.'"

But see, I didn't know any better.

Like Cosby, I got a shot at playing Las Vegas. Bobby Darin, a fan of mine from the clubs, signed me as the opening act for his three-week stint at the Flamingo Hotel. Bobby was cool. He could sing his ass off, and he was married to that pretty little girl Sandra Dee. And the $2,400 a week he offered to pay me was more monies than I'd ever made.

Maxine went with me, and once I arrived in Sin City, I fell in love with the bright lights, party-time atmosphere, and around-the-clock hustle of the Strip. Seeing my name on the Flamingo's marquee, in the same air as Sinatra and Sammy, was as big a thrill as I'd had up to that time. But the shows were something else. I knew I wasn't as good as the reviews said I was, and I knew why. I just didn't want to say it.

I didn't have to. One night Don Rickles came backstage and praised my act.

"It's uncanny," he said. "You sound just like Bill Cosby."

Shit.

Why'd he have to remind me?

13

IN LOS ANGELES, BOBBY DARIN THREW A PARTY IN MY HONOR AT a chi-chi Beverly Hills restaurant. The place was so fancy it made me nervous. I was even more uncomfortable being the center of attention, especially among all the famous people he'd invited. I sat across from Groucho Marx, who told me that he'd seen me on "The Merv Griffin Show" a few weeks earlier, when I'd guested with Jerry Lewis.

It hadn't been one of my better moments—Jerry and I had gotten laughs by spitting on each other, and Groucho, it turned out, had a few things to say about that.

"Young man, you're a comic?" he asked.

"Yes," I nodded. "Yes, I am."

"So how do you want to end up? Have you thought about that? Do you want a career you're proud of? Or do you want to end up a spitting wad like Jerry Lewis?"

The man was right. I wondered how he knew I was so unsure of myself.

"Huh?" I mumbled.

"Do you ever see plays?" he repeated.

"No," I answered.

"Do you ever read books?"

"No."

I could feel the stirrings of an identity crisis. It was coming on like the beginning of an acid trip. Groucho's comments spoke to me. "Wake up, Richard. Yes, you are an ignorant jerk, pimping your talent like a cheap whore. But you don't have to stay that way. You have a brain. Use it."

The thing was, I didn't have to. Sid Caesar eased me into movies. I met him at the Chateau Marmont Hotel in Hollywood. He interviewed me about being in *The Busy Body*, a loopy cops-and-gangsters picture he was about to start filming. Having grown up watching "Your Show of Shows," I was intimidated meeting Caesar, and also by having to keep up with his quick mind.

"I can do German," he said. "What about you?"

I stared at him and said to myself, "Goddamn, Sid Caesar's talking to me."

But apparently I said something good. Outside the hotel, my agent said, "You're going to play a detective."

The movie zipped by before I learned what I was supposed to do. On the set, I met fellow comics Dom DeLuise, Jan Murray, and Godfrey Cambridge, but otherwise I tiptoed around the cameras, lights, and shit while asking myself, "What the fuck am I doing here?"

As for acting, I faked it. Tried a little of this, a little of that. Some Steve McQueen, some Humphrey Bogart. Bless my confused heart. But it was hard because I didn't have my own thing to do.

Why, Richard? Why's that?

Because I didn't know shit about myself.

As soon as I finished, I went on a nightclub tour of the Midwest and dropped in on my family in Peoria in October. It was my first

trip back home since leaving five years earlier. Nothing had changed.
The places and people were the same.

Going home's nice. Some of the brothers still want to break my face.
"Nigger, you ain't shit. You wasn't shit when you were here. I seen you
do that shit on TV. That's the same shit you were doing around the
poolroom. It ain't nothing." Then a moment later: "Let me have a dollar."

I fell into the old routines. Playing cards. Fishing. Drinking.
Scootching whores. Slipping in shit and getting laughs.

"This will always be your home, baby," my grandma said.

Yet I'd changed. Or so I thought. I'd seen more. Seen possibilities.
Played for bigger pots.

When I'd left town originally nobody'd noticed. Now the *Peoria
Journal Star* wrote a story about me coming back and quoted my
dad saying that my success had done the family proud and even
"brought a tear or two."

That was nice, Dad.

How come we never talked like that in person?

Questions like that were probably what'd brought me back home
in the first place. Over the past five years, I'd become more successful than I'd ever imagined. I'd almost forgotten who the person
was who'd left Peoria. I'd lost my way when I decided to go for
the bucks.

I had to rediscover Richard Pryor, the Richard Pryor whom club
owner Harold Parker had allowed to pretend he could play the
piano and tell jokes, and then described as "having more nerve than
anybody I've ever seen."

But how?

By April 1967, Maxine was nine months pregnant and due almost any time. She wanted a commitment from me, something I had no intention of giving her.

I gambled. I stayed out all night at clubs. I could barely commit to being me. How could I give her more? But the more I said no, the more adamant she became. The only reason we stayed together was because neither of us had any other place to go.

We were stuck, and it wasn't fun.

One night, unable to stand the pressure any longer, I walked outside and stared up at the moon. It was like a big orange balloon. A big orange titty talking to me. "Hey, Rich, what's going on? Why don't you come and get me?" There was just something about it—the air, the vibes, the moon, the way it beckoned. I said, "Damn, this moon's got something to do with me."

So I went with it.

I jumped in my car and followed the moon.

I drove as if I was holding on to a rope, and when I finally let go I was in Tijuana, Mexico. For the next few days, I rested, drank, and partied with several pretty little whores, who showered me with loving attention and for a while had me forgetting Maxine.

The guards at the border weren't as nice. On my way back into the United States, they pulled me over and searched my car. I didn't look guilty, but I was black and I'm convinced that was the reason I got stopped. They searched me and said that they found an ounce of pot.

Bullshit.

There wasn't even enough to roll a joint.

But.

They busted me anyway.

So there I was. A black man going to jail for drugs as he tries crossing the U.S. border. It didn't look good for Richard, no, it didn't.

I was fucking terrified for my life, you know?

I was in jail in California. When they arrest you, they be serious. They'd look all in your asshole. You talk about degrading a nigger. That degrades you immediately. "Take off your clothes." I didn't know what they be looking for. "What you be looking for, man, in my ass?" There ain't nothing in my asshole. If I had a pussy, I might dig it. You can hide something in your pussy. But in my ass? What am I gonna hide in my asshole? A pistol?"

They threw me in a cell by myself, which was something of a relief. I laid down on the top bunk. Then they brought in another guy. Another black man. Unlike me, however, this dude was big and scary. I don't want to accuse nobody of being guilty of anything before they're tried, but I knew from looking at him that the world was a little safer with him behind bars.

But was I?

Without saying a word to me, without even acknowledging me, he stripped off all his clothes and walked around buck naked. He reminded me of an angry bull, brooding, snorting, grinding. I feared what was going to happen when he caught sight of my skinny ass. I thought, Christ, I'm going to have to knock this motherfucker out. God, please give me the strength or else I'm probably going to have to get fucked.

Eventually, he laid down on the bottom bunk and didn't bother me, and I didn't say shit to the man, either. Honest. I didn't even get off the top bunk. Not a peep from Rich.

Many hours later, a deputy looked in the cell and asked with genuine surprise what I was doing there.

Was he more ignorant than me?

"I was arrested," I said.

"Why are you still in here, though?" he asked.

Several possible responses came to mind, before I said, "They won't let me out."

"But you've got all this money."

In the panic and confusion of getting arrested and going to jail, I'd forgotten there was $7,500 in my pocket.

"You can get your ass out of here," he continued.

"Well, let me out, then," I said.

After posting bail, I got in my car and drove home and found out my daughter Elizabeth had been born. Congratulations, Rich. But you didn't care, did you?

Well, to be honest, not that much.

You know, my attitude about kids and fatherhood was something stupid, something selfish, something that put all of them after my own momentary concerns.

As she should have, Maxine resented me to the point where I was unable to take it anymore. I had a hard time thinking about anything but my own needs, and no matter how much she screamed and fought with me, I simply wasn't going to change.

It's nothing to be proud of. It's just the way it was.

Finally, the day came when it was just all-out war between us, and I said, "You know what? I could leave here."

Maxine didn't argue.

I remember that day. It was clear.

As I left, I felt like I could see all the way to tomorrow and the next day, you know?

14

I DON'T REMEMBER HOW THE SUMMER OF 1967 WAS FOR THE REST of the country, but my ass landed at the Sunset Tower Motel in Hollywood, home for a hodgepodge of Hollywood dreamers, schemers, and hustlers. For about $100 a month, I not only got a place to sleep but also an interesting social life.

For starters, the girl I dated lived there. Brandi worked as a phone operator, but moonlighted as a dancer at the Whiskey A Go-Go. Another dancer friend of hers, Carol, also lived in the Tower. The first time Brandi took me to Carol's apartment, I walked in and saw another guy in there. I said the first thing that came to mind, "Let's take off our clothes and have an orgy."

How was I supposed to know the other guy was Carol's brother? Paul Mooney, a large black man who loved to talk and talk and talk, would become a comedian, my lifelong friend, collaborator, comic foil, alter ego, antagonist, and so on.

But as soon as Mooney heard me suggest having a sex party, he exploded. He threw my ass out in the hall.

"Get the fuck out, nigger," he said as the door closed behind me.

Mooney and I began seeing each other at comedy clubs, and we became friends anyway. He was fascinated by me. He always said he'd never known anyone who didn't give a shit about rules or propriety. Someone who didn't care about anything except what he wanted at that moment.

That was me—especially once I discovered instant gratification through a drug dealer I called Dirty Dick. He was a funny-looking black dude who talked in bullshit rhymes. Handled top-of-the-line cocaine. I used the motherfucker as if he was an automatic teller machine, snorting up $100-$200 a day. And I didn't even realize how much I liked to snort coke.

After one night with Dick, I came home fairly well fucked up. Not a great idea in the building where I lived because it was a strange place if you weren't careful. For instance, the elevator had a mind of its own. If you pushed 3, you ended up in the basement. If you pushed basement, you were fucked.

So while I was attempting to navigate a path to my apartment, something happened between me and the motherfucker working the late shift at the front desk. I don't know what, but it was loud and nasty.

"You can't say that crap to me," he said.

"If I want, I can say it to you *and* your mama," I snapped.

In a blur, this motherfucker turned into Bruce Lee with a bad attitude. He snapped his shoes off, crouched in a karate stance, started waving his fists and snarled, "Come on, nigger. Come on and try it."

I thought the motherfucker was funny. He moved way too much to know something. Police records indicated that I hit the motherfucker in the face and broke his glasses.

I don't remember shit about that.

But then the cops arrived, only I didn't know they were cops, and when they slapped some handcuffs on me, I thought something strange was going down. I thought maybe I might be going for a swim with the fishies. Held in front of the hotel, I shouted toward the building and passing cars, "Hey, y'all, help me! They're taking me someplace. Help me!"

I was high, crazy.

I went to jail. Then the fucker sued and won $75,000.

What could I do?

I just said, "Fuck it."

◆   ◆   ◆

Then Maxine sued me for child support and assorted bullshit. She claimed that we'd lived together like husband and wife. I didn't contest it, and the court sided with her. I tried to avoid the mess by shuffling from one club to the next.

In a way, I used that to my advantage. I saw myself as a victim of the system, an outsider for whom justice was out of reach, a dream, and then I saw how closely my situation mirrored the black man's larger struggle for dignity and equality and justice in white society.

That was me.

I was that character.

That was the person to whom I had to give voice.

I decided to drop out of the whole damn thing altogether. Got rid of my driver's license. Quit carrying identification of any kind. Stopped using banks, paying traffic tickets, income taxes, and all that shit.

Why not?

I couldn't win. It didn't seem as if any of us could win.

I saw the judge give one nigger forty years. He said, "That's right, fella. Forty years. You want more time, buddy?"

Dude had a court-appointed lawyer, right. Copping a plea. "Your Honor, this man is not a heroin dealer per se. He's being manipulated by these people. He was merely trying to get enough monies together to help his dear mom. She had a spinal condition. She needed an operation, and she didn't have the funds to do this. He was merely trying to raise the money. He tried every odd job he could, and he couldn't have raised the money. When the officers caught him with the 280 kilos, he was trying to purchase a hospital in the Bahamas."

Judge said, "Motion denied."

Nigger was so fucked up when they laid him away, he said, "Thank you, Your Honor."

At our last meeting, my agent sounded like one of my grandmother's whores singing to a john. "You're great, baby. Oh, you're the best. No one else like you, baby." The money was getting bigger. Checks piled up around my place like litter on the highway. I didn't have to worry about work.

My agent booked me at the Aladdin in Las Vegas. It was a big deal. I was nonplussed. In fact, as we shook hands, I had the feeling that I was making a pact with someone who just wanted to suck my blood.

Hey, man! Say, nigger. You with the cape. What you doing peeking in them people's window? What's you name, boy?

Dracula?

What kind of a name is that for a nigger? Where you from, fool?

Transylvania?

I know where that is, nigger. Yeah. You ain't the smartest motherfucker in the world, you know. Even though you is the ugliest. Oh, yeah. Why don't you get your teeth fixed, nigger?

I couldn't explain the transformation taking place. I don't understand it myself. I only know my days of pretending to be as slick and colorless as Cosby were numbered. There was a world of junkies and winos, pool hustlers and prostitutes, women and family screaming inside my head, trying to be heard. The longer I kept them bottled up, the harder they tried to escape. The pressure built till I went nuts.

Better get home before the sun come up. See your ass in the day, you're liable to get arrested!

By the time I rolled into Vegas in September, I was completely fucked up, okay on the outside, but I felt as if my legs were going to give out any minute. I was sandwiched between the headliner, Pat the "Hip Hypnotist" Collins, and the Brasilia Jazz Review. Or so people have told me, because I don't remember shit.

Only that it was opening night.

"Now, please welcome a very funny gentleman. You've seen him on a number of TV shows. Mr. Richard Pryor."

I came out. Nice applause.

I looked at the audience. The first person I saw was Dean Martin, seated at one of the front tables. He was staring right back at me.

At me!

I asked myself, Who's he looking at, Rich?

I checked out the rest of the audience. They were staring at me as intently as Dean, waiting for that first laugh.

Again, I asked myself, Who're they looking at, Rich?

I didn't know.

I couldn't say, They're looking at you, Richard, because I didn't know who Richard Pryor was. And in that flash of introspection when I was unable to find an answer, I crashed. I had a nervous breakdown.

I looked back at Dean, who was still looking at me, waiting for something, you know?

You want to suck what? Nigger, are you some kind of pervert? An ugly pervert. You ain't sucking nothing here, junior. You want to suck some blood, go down to the blood bank, nigger. Hope you get sickle cell.

I imagined what I looked like and got disgusted. I gasped for clarity as if it was oxygen. The fog rolled in. In a burst of inspiration, I finally spoke to the sold-out crowd: "What the fuck am I doing here?"

Then I turned and walked off the stage.

God was much funnier than me that night.

Instead of guiding me offstage to my dressing room, He pointed me in the wrong direction. I found myself standing on a narrow ledge behind the curtain. I couldn't turn around. Nor would I. So in my tux, I inched and clawed my way along the tiny lip of wood, toward the faint glow of an exit sign, scraping my nose until it bled and muttering, "Fuck, fuck, fuck…"

Backstage, I gathered my clothes and left the hotel, climbed into my '65 Mustang, and drove to L.A.

My agent was hysterical, incredulous. How could I have walked off? What the fuck was going on?

"Do you know what you did?" my agent screamed. "Do you know what this means?"

"No, you're the agent. You tell me."

Then I heard those famous words.

"You'll never work in this town again. Did you hear me? You will never work in this town again!"

I have a thing for nudity. I always like to get naked. I did that in Vegas. Got naked and ran through the casino nude. Jumped up on the table and said, "Blackjack!"

I can still here him saying that.

YOU WILL NEVER WORK IN THIS TOWN AGAIN!

15

CONTRARY TO RUMOR, MY LAS VEGAS FLAMEOUT WASN'T IN front of a Mafia audience. It didn't cause the mob to put out a contract on me, lead to a ban from ever performing at the hotels, or serve as my ticket to the loony bin.

The only fact was the inevitability. The breakdown was the only way I could shed the phony image I'd created and start building my self-respect.

I was a Negro for twenty-three years. I gave that shit up. No room for advancement.

In the weeks after, I continued to hear the threat: "You'll never work in this town again."

So.

It would've been a different story if my agent had said, "You'll never fuck in this town again."

Then I would've listened.

As it happened, after returning to L.A., I fell hard in love with Shelley Bonus, a rich hippie girl who would become my second wife. We met at a nightclub. Shelley noticed me looking at her, strolled over to where I sat, and then kicked up her leg as if finishing a dance step.

That was so goddamn cute. I was hooked immediately.

There's nothing better or more exciting than falling in love, and, if I do say so, I do it well. However, it's like jumping in a pool when you don't know how to swim.

I hear myself screaming, "Edge! Rich, get to the edge!"

And so it was with Shelley.

We didn't waste any time getting together. She moved into my rustic cabinlike place above Laurel Canyon, and we fell passionately, madly, silly in love. She walked around barefoot, wore love beads, lighted incense, knew things, and at a time when I was struggling, she made me feel free.

Her simplicity was charming. We could do absolutely nothing and be happy. We used to walk around, picking up rocks and giving them names. We kissed them. We gave them to each other as presents. Stupid shit that made us laugh.

Then we got married. It was really fun, man. All those funny things we used to do together. I'd bring her a rock. She'd go, "Oh, a rock. For me?"

She got me to marry her while we was balling and I was coming.

"Will you marry me?"

"Yes! Yeah! Oh, yeah!"

At the end of December, my dad called with bad news. My step-mother Viola had died. I told him I was sorry and hoped that was enough. But he wanted me at the funeral.

"Dad, I ain't going," I said.

I couldn't imagine dealing with all the family shit.

"That's all right, son," he said. "You don't have to come. But the next time you be on 'Ed Sullivan,' it'll be a duo."

"What do you mean?"

He said, "It'll be you telling jokes and me kicking your ass."

That made me laugh. But I knew he meant it.

A few hours later, my Aunt Dee called to check on whether or not I had any sense at all.

I said, "Yes, tell Dad I'm coming home, but only because I don't want him kicking my ass on 'Ed Sullivan.'"

My dad was very broken up when I got there. Everybody else talked about the weather.

We were going to my stepmother's funeral. It was one of the coldest days in the history of Peoria, Illinois. Like twenty below zero. I'm sitting in the back seat with my father, crying and shit, and I say, "Pop, it's all right. Hey, man, it's gonna be okay."

He said, "Man, it get any colder, I'm gonna have to bury the bitch myself."

That's my father. I'm not lying. He'd be at the graveyard, talking to the preacher. "Say, man, when's the shit over? Goddamn. Get to the part about the date. Shit, I love you, baby. But shit, goddamn, it's cold out here."

Paul Mooney started taking me to Redd Foxx's club located in Central Los Angeles. It was the right place for me at the right time. With a black audience, I was free to experiment with material that was more natural. It was frightening, since I didn't know myself and had to learn who I was. It was like I was there but I wasn't there, you know.

Yet it was also lovely, comfortable. I talked about the black man's struggle to make it in a white world, which was also my struggle. For the first time since I began to perform at Harold's Club, I saw black people laughing—not just at cute shit. They laughed at the people I knew. The people they knew. It was enlightening.

None more so than Redd Foxx himself. Redd was a player, a hard player from the old school. He carried a switchblade. Sometimes a gun. He ran the club like a gangster, treating friends like relatives and enemies with scorn. People were beat up regularly. Redd also liked the cocaine, too. I spent many nights when I felt as if we were in the coke Olympics.

But Redd was a mesmerizing storyteller—the best ones always concerned his friend Malcolm X. Not only did listening to that shit fascinate me, it sparked a fire inside my brain. It was an awakening. Malcolm was a bad motherfucker, Redd said, but he also took care of business. He was proud, brilliant, sincere, passionate, dedicated to teaching about human beings, about being human.

"In the early days, Malcolm hated what he called the white devil," Redd explained. "Then he realized that we were all different shades of the same stick. The motherfucker got killed for it."

It was the same evolution that I'd go through. Strangely, I hadn't been affected by Malcolm X's death when it occurred. However, after Redd introduced me to him as a person and what he stood for, I missed him terribly.

A few months later, Martin Luther King, Jr., was assassinated outside his Memphis motel room. I was in Chicago that day. I watched the news on the TV in my hotel room and tried to understand the loss. I couldn't.

Neither could I make any sense of Robert Kennedy's murder two months later in Los Angeles. At the time, I was walking down a hotel corridor in Washington, D.C. It must've been right after the shooting. Ed Sullivan passed me rushing in the opposite direction. Something seemed wrong. He didn't stop or say hi. He seemed in a daze. Moments later, after I turned on the TV, I was overtaken by that same glassy confusion.

The good good ones were being bumped off.

John, Malcolm, Martin and Bobby.

What to make of it?

I wanted to understand why that shit had happened. But there was no way. It was part of a whole collage of shit that I couldn't get a grip on. I probably wasn't alone in that respect, though I sure felt like it.

In early 1968, I worked at the Village Gate in New York, one of the few clubs that didn't object to the new material I was performing, which the more conservative bookers considered inflammatory, crude, and in some cases obscene. (And to think I was just starting to find myself.) Going there gave me the opportunity to meet actress Shelley Winters, who came backstage and asked if I'd be in her next movie, *Wild in the Streets*.

"I don't know," I said. "But I'll try."

The money aspect interested me, but far more important at the time was meeting jazz great Miles Davis, who was the club's headliner. Though our paths hadn't crossed, Miles and I were brothers waiting to meet. Kindred spirits. Before we even spoke, he did something that no one else would've done, because no one would've understood the shit I was going through without a detailed explanation.

But Miles' radar picked me up like a lost plane. About half an hour before the show, he had one of his guys come to my dressing room and tell me the lineup had changed.

"Miles is gonna play first," he said.

"What?" I asked, wondering what the fuck was going on.

"Miles is going to open. Then you follow."

The gesture was pure Miles—intuitive, supportive, generous, and in sync with the moment. By trading places, he was giving me a vote of support. Beyond that, he was leading me to the edge of the diving board. He knew that I was frightened, and he knew I thought the jump was hard. But he also knew that I could do it if given a nudge. I just had to believe in myself.

Be brave, he was telling me.

Be true to your own self.

Listen to the music inside your head, Rich. Play with your heart.

After the show Miles invited me to his dressing room. When I entered he was kissing Dizzy Gillespie, with tongue and shit, which made me wonder what kind of shit he had planned for me.

But Miles played a different tune with me. We got in a cab and went to a midtown apartment where he introduced me to a woman I called the Gypsy Lady. She was dark and mysterious, with eyes as hot as fire, and she had the best cocaine I ever tried. It was a big motherfucking rock. Like the Hope Diamond. We chopped and snorted until the sun crept through the windows and then we disappeared like vampires.

"From now on, you get your coke from her," Miles said as we left. "She's got the best."

After that evening, our lives became intertwined, my Miles' and mine. I played his music, collected his art, admired his independence, understood his rudeness, and loved the way he talked. That was probably the best thing about Miles. That voice. It fascinated me like nothing else. No matter what he said, Miles sounded cool.

Those shows marked the beginning of my transformation into Richard Pryor again, though change was not without its price. I didn't act as if

I was married. I hung out till all hours at nightclubs. I indulged my appetite for drugs and booze and jive. I let temptation serve as my muse.

I wasn't close to being normal. I couldn't stop drinking till the bartender said, "We got no more fucking liquor."

I had no conscience. One night Mooney brought April, a beautiful sportswriter, to Shelley's and my little cabin in the hills, and as with any attractive female, I wanted her, chased her, I got down on my hands and knees and begged and then I went off with her. Shit, did Shelley ever want to strangle me.

I couldn't stop myself even after Shelley became pregnant in the fall of 1968, but then I didn't see myself as clearly as others did. I remember Redd Foxx and I spent an entire night and most of the next morning at a little table in his club, battling each other for the attention of a sexy waitress, listening to jazz, and snorting cocaine by the spoonful. I kept asking for more, more, more, and Redd kept giving it to me, until finally I was too tired to inhale.

"Hey, Redd, why do I always want more?" I asked.

He laughed as if to emphasize my ignorance.

"Because you're a junkie."

Then it was my turn to laugh.

"Bullshit."

I just didn't see it.

Later, when I finally went home, Shelley was waiting for me and she wasn't happy.

"You don't love anybody, do you?" she asked.

"I love Miles," I said.

That wasn't exactly true.

At the end of September, while I was working on the movie *Wild in the Streets*, my father died. I was still in bed when the phone rang. Shelley and I ignored it. But the ringing continued as if that phone was screaming, "Get the fuck up and answer me, motherfucker." Shelley got it.

"Richard, it's your grandmother," she said.

"Hello, Marie…"

He'd been with five women. Five!

At the same time.

In the midst of it, his heart gave out.

Shit.

I want to die like my father. He died fucking. He was fifty-seven. The woman was eighteen. He came and went at the same time.

Didn't nobody cry at his funeral. Everybody just said, "Lucky motherfucker."

And nobody else would fuck the woman for two years. "I don't want none of that pussy. No, thank you."

I hugged Shelley for a long time. Needed her strength as tears ran from my eyes.

"The king is dead," I finally muttered. "Long live the king."

Shelley traveled with me to Peoria, where I was immediately overwhelmed by the pull of family.

"You can never escape, can you?" I asked myself. "Not even when you die."

My dad lived in a nice house that he'd bought several years earlier with twenty grand in cash that I'd handed him one night following a Chicago club date. A lot of shit went down inside me when I walked through that door and he wasn't there.

My whole family was gathered there. The place was packed. Still, I felt an unmistakable absence.

Daddy.

"Your father fucked everything," my Aunt Maxine said. "Just be glad he didn't fuck you."

Okay.

Tender thought.

My grandmother, who had already taken over his house, chose me to go to the funeral parlor and pick out the casket. I didn't want to do it. I was his child, his baby. Inside, I cried, "Why, Mama? I don't want to."

But who else was there?

I was the only son.

I was the only one with monies.

Well, I picked out something that seemed like him. Nothing fancy. Nothing crazy. Just a casket.

When I got back home, they gave me the worst shit. Why'd you get that? What kind of casket is that? Did you try to save money? Didn't they have anything fancier? This is your father, after all. Shit, I didn't know what to say. It was as if they were beating me up because they didn't know what else to do.

Thank God for Shelley. She came to my defense.

"Damn it, you all shouldn't have done that to him," she yelled. "He went down there. He went through the pain. He did his best. None of you offered to help."

There was silence. Stunned motherfucking silence. Because no one dared talk back to Marie. But Shelley did. And everybody knew she was right. Because of her outburst, that day became very important to me. It didn't mean I loved anybody less, but in a way it freed me some. Loosened those chains.

Shelley flew home before the funeral. Since my father wasn't Catholic, the service was held in St. Patrick's gymnasium on October 4, 1968. He was buried in St. Joseph's Cemetery later that day. I didn't think it would hit me as hard as it did.

White people love their dearly departed, but their funerals be different. They don't give it up easy. They hold that shit in until they get home. Then they cry softly, "Ah-hoo, boo-hoo, ah!"

But black people let it hang out. "Whaaaaaaaaaaaaaaaaa!" Then they fall on your ass. They don't ever faint. They just lean on your ass. You have to carry them to the car. "Say, bitch, get up. Damn, you got to get on me 'cuz that motherfucker's dead?"

My grandmother yelled like that. Scared the shit out of you at a funeral. "Whaaaaaaaaaaaa!"

I said, "What's the matter, Mama?" I thought maybe my dad had raised up or something.

Naw, he was dead. The odd thing was, now that he lay dead, I couldn't stop talking to him. You know, inside my head. Conversation flowed, man. But when he was alive, I don't think we ever really talked. No "Hey, Dad, can I ask you" shit. No passing on stories or advice. Most of the time, he'd come into the room, say some stuff, and I'd go, "Yes, sir." Even as a man.

One time I got tired of my dad kicking my ass. I had a fight with him in the front yard. Well, it wasn't exactly a fight. I did the best I could. I said, "Man, I'm tired of taking these ass whippings. I ain't taking no fucking more. And that's it."

"What're you a man now, motherfucker?"

"Yeah, okay."

And he hit me in the chest so hard that my chest just caved in and wrapped around his fist and held it there.

I looked at my dad one last time. Wearing his best suit. I put a little money in his pocket.

Hey, Dad, just in case there's any action up there.

16

WATCHING TELEVISION, WHICH SUPPOSEDLY PUTS YOUR BRAIN to sleep, has always had the opposite effect on me. Paul Mooney and I used to yell at the shows as if the actors could hear us. The shit was so stupid that it was funny. I knew I could write much better.

I always wondered why they never have a black hero on any of the shows. I always wanted to go to the movies and see a black hero. I figured maybe someday they'll have it on television, man. (Some funky music plays and then):
   "Look! Up in the sky!
   "It's a crow!
   "It's a bat!
   "No, it's Super Nigger!"

As with so many ideas hatched in living rooms beneath clouds of dope smoke, mine sounded crazy but brilliant. Instead of a television show, I was going to make a movie. I'd write, direct, produce, and star. Since Hollywood wasn't overflowing with opportunities for black actors, Paul and I would create our own opportunity.

It sounded so simple that it seemed possible.

"We'll get our friends together and do it," I said.

"Where we getting the money?" he asked.

"Me," I said. "I'll put it up. I'll produce."

"Who's gonna direct?"

"Me."

"Who's gonna be in it?"

"Everybody we know."

"Oh, shit."

We began shooting *Bon Appétit* in March 1969. Penelope Spheeris, a successful director now, was the camera operator because she had gone to film school. But that's as much legitimacy as the film had.

The picture opened with a black maid having her pussy eaten at the breakfast table by the wealthy white man who owned the house where she worked. Then, a gang of Black Panther types burst into the house and took him prisoner. As he was led away, the maid fixed her dress and called, "*Bon appétit*, baby!"

The rest of the movie, which was retitled *The Trial*, was a silly stab at a political statement. The Panthers held the guy in a basement and put him on trial for all the racial crimes in U.S. history. *Black Caesar*, *Superfly*, and *Cleopatra Jones* hadn't come out. I thought we were breaking new ground. But halfway through the editing process, we ran out of money. To keep the dream alive, I borrowed money from a shady character I knew. Eventually I brought in a few more people like him. Then there was a falling-out. The unfinished print was stolen. I bought it back. And then it disappeared again.

It was a better story than the film itself.

One day Paul saw the film advertised as a coming attraction at a downtown art house. After some investigation, I managed to reacquire the print, which still wasn't completed. In a last-ditch effort, I persuaded Bill Cosby to put up money for a final edit. Then he and I watched the final print. He said only one thing, "Hey, this shit is weird."

I agreed. The movie was strange. Too strange. Even for me. Despite the effort, I shelved the print and learned a lesson. To make a movie from start to finish, you need a good reason.

I just ran out of them.

There was one successful production that summer. On July 16, 1969, the day the Apollo 11 astronauts lifted off, Shelley gave birth to our daughter, Rain. She was the first of my three children to arrive when I was in a state where I could welcome her. I just wasn't sure about the rest of the world. After Rain was born, a nurse told me she had to fill out a birth record and asked what she was.

"A human being," I said.

The nurse, irritated, asked the question again, this time adding, "Is she black or white?"

"I already told you," I responded. "She's a human being. Just write that on your goddamn form."

I didn't know anyone more aware of their image than Billy Dee Williams, who I met on the TV pilot "Carter's Army." Suave and handsome, he was also very serious about his career and what people thought of him. Mooney and I played poker at his house, but he didn't like hanging out with us anywhere else. He worried that we were going to get him in trouble.

I didn't remotely identify with that worrywart shit. My life was populated by characters. There was Prophet, a moody but talented painter. Dirty Dick. A whole circus of hustlers, whores, winos, and hangers-on. I thought they were people who knew stuff worth knowing. But then I've never claimed to be a great judge of character, you know?

I did slightly better with pets. Shelley and I, renting Redd Foxx's house at the time, filled it with a menagerie of creatures, including a couple of Afghan hounds, some lovebirds, and fish. Mooney gave me a squirrel monkey, who I named Boyfriend. We got along okay. I even thought he kinda liked me more than was normal for a monkey.

I named it Friend. Because the first time I opened the cage, he ran up my arm and stuck his dick in my ear. It felt like a wet Q-tip. And when there wasn't no action for him, he got mad and pissed all over my cheek. I grabbed the motherfucker and threw him up to the ceiling. He grabbed the chandelier and laughed.

"Thought you had me, didn't ya?"

I felt sorry for Boyfriend. As I watched him swing through his cage, he seemed lonely. So I bought him a friend, a female squirrel monkey who I called Girlfriend.

I got him a beautiful little woman. I called her Sister. And he did the same thing to her. He ran right in the cage and stuck his dick in her ear. She said, "Freeze. First thing I gotta do is show you where the pussy's at."

And then he got some monkey pussy and went crazy.

Mooney, who begrudgingly watched the animals whenever Shelley and I went out of town, resigned his caretaker post once I added Girlfriend to the mix. In need of a new babysitter for several weeks, I pressed Dirty Dick into service. He was my only option. Still, I should've known better.

When I got back, both of the monkeys were dead.

"They killed themselves," he said. "Committed suicide."

"What?" I asked, shocked.

"Yeah," he said, pointing to a gas burner on the old stove in the middle of his kitchen. "They accidentally turned it on and suffocated."

I thought he killed them on purpose. Distraught, I went home and cried. Shelley didn't understand why I was taking it so hard and asked me to cry outside. As I sat grieving, the mean German shepherd from next door hopped the fence. Normally, he terrorized the monkeys, but he seemed forlorn too and put his head in my lap.

I felt something pushing my hand. I looked down and he said, "Hey, Rich, what's the matter?"

"My monkeys is dead. They died."

He said, "What? Your monkeys is dead? You mean the ones that used to be in the trees? Damn, I was going to eat them, too."

Then he said, "Life's a bitch, ain't it? One day you're here, the next day you're gone. Well, don't linger on it. You know, that shit can get to you."

"Thank you."

He went away, walked to the fence, and got ready to jump over. He turned around and said, "You know I'm gonna be chasing you tomorrow."

The monkeys weren't the only casualty. Shelley and I weren't going to make it much longer. The sparks were gone. We fought constantly. Mooney referred to our place as "the House of Pain." Instead of giving each other pet rocks, now we threw them at each other.

My wife and I had a lot of fun for a long time. But she had this girlfriend. With big titties. You know the type I'm talking about. You try to ignore them for six months. Then she'd come into the house and you say, "Hello, there. How're you doing? No, I don't really notice your tits."

One day my wife came home and said she left her wallet over at her house. I ran. "I'll get it!"

Then I got the guilties. I had to tell her. 'Cause I thought she knew when she asked, "Have you seen Ethel?"

"I did it!"

"Did what?"

"Fucked Ethel."

"You fucked Ethel?"

She went and kicked Ethel's ass.

As Shelley and my fighting became fiercer and more frequent, I took increasing refuge at Dirty Dick's. In good times I had spent much of my time buying cocaine and shooting the shit with the lowlifes, whores, and addicts who were always at Dirty Dick's. Now I spent even more in his den of debauchery.

Shelley knew what went on up there. She hated Dick, and she hated how much time I spent hiding out with him. Periodically, she threatened to follow me to his house. Go there with me. Participate in the games. But I kept it off limits. The place was too nasty for her. It was also mine.

"I don't want you up there," I once said. "It's no place for you."

"Well, then come home," she said. "Spend more time with your family."

What did you think, Rich?

Yeah, right.

That's why I was up there, you know? I didn't want to spend time with my family. Didn't want to spend time with myself. Didn't want to spend time.

Wanted to buy me some time.

"I will," I said. "Just give me one more night. I need one more night."

Good, Rich. Why'd she believe you?

You think she did?

No.

Because one more night turned into dozens more. Couldn't help myself.

Like Redd Foxx said, I was a junkie.

No matter what I promised, once was never enough.

Shelley was smart. She knew that.

One night she went up to Dirty Dick's to find me and drag my doped-out ass back home, where I had promised to leave it. Only I wasn't at Dirty Dick's that night. I was getting high someplace else. Hanging with some other characters of ill repute, I'm sure. But the fact that Shelley had crossed into Dirty Dick's shadowy world made me crazy with anger and paranoia and jealousy.

Knowing the sordid shit she would be exposed to at Dirty Dick's, I should've been more concerned about Shelley. Worried. Protective. Ready to apologize and admit my wrongdoing. Instead, I thought, Why is she doing this to me?

What right does the bitch have? Telling me what to do?

What the hell was she doing anyway?

I got pissed. You know.

You be in love you don't want nobody in your puss. Especially when you find one that fits. I don't want no motherfucker stretching your pussy out.

The trouble was this: I didn't want to admit the truth. Shelley and I were history. We just hadn't reached the finish line yet. We still had to limp down the final stretch, shouting at each other and fighting as if that would help.

Heartache is like an education for a man. We don't really grow up until a woman breaks your fucking heart. That's your diploma. If you come through that, Jack, you're a man.

My first comedy album, recorded live at the Troubadour, didn't quite measure up to my favorites. I had loved Bob Newhart's first recording so much that I'd pilfered it from a little store in Peoria. Bill Cosby's debut album was perfect, perfectly hilarious. And in my mind, nobody, to this day, has made an album as brilliantly funny as Lenny Bruce's *Lima, Ohio*.

Mine was a good, though uneven, effort. Routines like "Super Nigger" revealed the voice that was trying to break through. A point of view was percolating beneath the surface. I just didn't know enough to put all the pieces together.

For the cover, I took off my clothes and parodied the cover of *National Geographic*, though when I think back on the day I was photographed I don't remember going native as much as I do the way Shelley went after me. During the shoot, Sonny Stinson, my old friend from Harold's Club, showed up. Shelley saw us hugging and went ballistic. Worse, she beat the shit out of me.

"What the fuck is wrong?" I yelled.

But I knew. I was affectionate to everyone but her. She was right. I deserved the beating.

I just didn't want to take it, you know.

And that was it. The end.

We find Super Nigger, with his X-ray vision that enables him to see through everything except Whitey, disguised as Clark Washington, mild-mannered custodian for the Daily Planet. *He's shuffling into Perry White's office.*

"Hey, man, I'm quitting, baby."

"Great Caesar's Ghost! I can't talk to you now."

"Talk to me, Jack. 'Cuz I'm ready to quit, man. You dig? I'm tired of doing them halls. Every time I finish, Lois Lane and them come slipping and sliding down through there and I got to do them over again. You dig it, baby? I'm through."

With an arrest warrant issued against me for failure to pay child support to Maxine and with Shelley wanting to kill me, I had more than enough motivation to get the hell out of Dodge. My life was a mess. It was as if I was stuck to a funnel cloud that was tearing a path of destruction everywhere I went. I sensed catastrophe around the corner and knew I had to get out.

One day Mooney and I got in my car and aimed the mother-fucker north. I wanted to go to Berkeley. I don't know why there, except I had it in my head.

For eight hours we drove up Interstate 5, drinking cheap wine and singing Motown songs at the top of our voices. When we ran out of songs, we made up new ones.

Obnoxious, loud, drunk, and exhausted, we rolled into the red-hot center of the counterculture as if late for a party.

I didn't have a single notion of what I was going to do, but being there felt right.

"I can't talk to you now," Perry White says to janitor Clark Washington. "The warehouse is on fire!"

"What warehouse?"

"Warehouse 86."

"Damn. That's where I got my stash. This looks like a job for Super Nigger!"

17

I SETTLED INTO A LIFE THAT WAS DRASTICALLY DIFFERENT FROM the comfortable but miserable one I'd fled. I rented a small, one-bedroom house for $110 a month. I bought a bed, threw it on the floor, and stuck a TV by it.

Don't tell Martha Stewart, but that was it. I was done with the furnishings.

I thought it was nice, though. Ghetto chic.

Such austerity was necessary. If I was going to find my lost soul, I needed to cast off everything but the bare essentials. I had to renounce the past in order to discover the future. House, car, clothes, women, friends—I tossed them all away. No one knew where I was, and no one got in unless I wanted them to.

It was the freest time of my life. Berkeley was a circus of exciting, extreme, colorful, militant ideas. Drugs. Hippies. Black Panthers. Antiwar protests. Experimentation. Music, theater, poetry. I was like a lightning rod. I absorbed bits of everything while forging my own uncharted path.

I indulged every thought that popped into my sick head. I read and reread a copy of Malcolm X's collected speeches. I put Marvin Gaye's song "What's Going On" on my stereo and played it so often it became the soundtrack for my life up there.

"What's goin' on?" Marvin would sing.

"Fuck if I know," I'd answer.

In a city of spectacles, I became one myself. I shambled in and out of coffeehouses in an old kimono, sandals, and a tall, cone-shaped hat that made me look like a deranged wizard. My sense of humor was equally bizarre. Some nights at clubs such as Basin Street West, Mandrake's, and the Showcase, I just made strange animal noises. Other nights I repeated a single word like "bitch" or "mother-fucker," but gave it fifty-seven different inflections.

Each outing was like playing jazz, searching for that one perfect note that would carry me into a higher state of bliss. I never thought about what I was going to do until I did it. Sometimes I stunk. Sometimes I surprised myself. But I went with whatever happened, you know.

As a result, I became braver, more confident, and willing to tap into whatever provocative or controversial thoughts I had. During one such performance, I repeated the most offensive, humiliating, disgraceful, distasteful, ugly, and nasty word ever used in the context of black people. The word embodied the hatred of racism as well as a legacy of self-hate.

Nigger.

And so this one night I decided to make it my own.

Nigger.

I decided to take the sting out of it.

Nigger.

As if saying it over and over again would numb me and every-body else to its wretchedness.

Nigger.

Said it over and over like a preacher singing hallelujah.

Hello, I'm Richard Pryor. I'm a nigger.

Nigger. Nigger. Nigger.
Niggerniggerniggerniggerniggernigger.

Maybe you didn't notice, you know. Because they didn't tell me till I was eight years old.

Saying it changed me, yes it did. It gave me strength, let me rise above shit.

Faster than a bowl of chitlins. Able to leap slums in a single bound.

Honest. It made me feel free to say it.
Clean.
It was the truth.
That's all I was looking to say. The truth.

I'm glad I'm black. I'd hate to be white. 'Cuz y'all got to go to the moon.
Ain't no niggers going to the moon, you know that. First of all, there ain't no niggers qualified. Or so you all tell us.
If niggers was hip, they'd help y'all get to the moon.
"Hey, let's organize and help them white motherfuckers get to the moon."
"So they leave us alone!"

Among my discoveries in Berkeley was an extremely passionate, highly charged, supersophisticated renaissance of black intellectual, artistic, and political activity. It was fueled by the minds and fervor of stars like activist Angela Davis and novelist Ishmael Reed, who were smart, proud, committed … and uncompromisingly black.

The bunch I knew could also party their ass off. Cecil Brown, who wrote the novel *The Life and Loves of Mr. Jiveass Nigger*, told some of the earthiest, most entertaining stories ever around 3 a.m. Through Cecil, I met Claude Brown, the author of *Manchild in the Promised Land*, and Reed, who impressed me as one of the most honest people I've met.

By comparison, I was uneducated and ignorant, though listening to their ideas inspired me just as Malcolm X's writings had. I wanted to do something. One night I served as the disc jockey on a radio station, playing Miles and rambling on about Nixon, the Vietnam War, the Black Panthers, and shit. I didn't know anything about that shit. But who better to talk about it?

Then I got the idea I could write. For a time, I holed up in my house and wrote. Fueled by coke, coffee, cigarettes, and alcohol, I cranked out page after page of stories containing ideas and opinions that I thought were important.

"I'm a serious motherfucker," I told myself.

Finally, I got the guts to show my work to Reed. He sent it back with the note, "Man, dis ain't my language."

Well, that stopped my attempt at serious writing cold.

He could've said, "Motherfucker, you can't write."

But he made it hard. He was cold and, as I said, honest.

I heard that Shelley was hanging out with Miles. I don't think they were lovers. But just that they were spending time together messed me up.

Women get their heart broke, they cry.

Men don't do that. Men hold it in like it don't hurt. They walk around and get hit by trucks.

"Didn't he see that truck?"

"Man, he wouldn't have seen a 747. His heart was broke."

I was so pissed off about Shelley and Miles that I walked into a pawnshop, bought a trumpet, and blew it on a street corner outside an Italian restaurant. Only I didn't know how to play the trumpet. Not a fucking note. But I blew the motherfucker as if the shrill, discordant sounds that went screaming into the darkness would let everyone know how unhappy I felt inside.

Then Bill Cosby, of all people, walked out of the restaurant to see who was playing such shit. He had to have figured it was someone real avant-garde or a terrorist. He looked stunned to see me.

"Man, what are you doing?" he asked.

"Playing the trumpet."

"No, you aren't," he said. "You're making everybody in the restaurant sick."

Bill invited me to join him inside, where he was eating with two of the tallest, prettiest white women I'd ever seen. I thought, Damn, wouldn't you know. But after a while, one of those Amazon beauties gently stroked my leg underneath the table. I looked across the table at Bill and said to myself, "Sick, my ass. Man, that trumpet shit worked."

Berkeley was full of characters worse than me, and I seemed to get tangled up with all of them. I hung out with a coke dealer named Haywood who lived by the water in Sausalito. He once gave me a samurai sword.

"Here, man, cut off your head," he said encouragingly. "Do the honorable thing."

I also remember Geena, this hippie chick, whose entire self-worth centered around a pair of satin shoes Janis Joplin had given her. One night, in a fit of downright cruelty, I threw those shoes into the Bay.

Sweet Jesus was a pimp who controlled everything.

And I still shudder at the thought of Crazy Mary, a whore who had wooden teeth. I made a grave error with her once. I gave her money.

In her eyes that made us something.

She followed me around town. She showed up at clubs while I was on stage. She raised tons of hell.

"Where is he?" she screamed in a voice that ripped through even the noisiest nightclubs. "Where the hell is my Richard?"

One time she barged into the bathroom while I was inside doing my business. I kicked the door shut. She pushed it open again with her shoulder. I smashed it shut again and told her to get the fuck away.

"Open this goddamn door right now!" she yelled.

"No."

"Why not? You're just shitting. Everybody shits."

Crazy Mary scared me. She wanted to fuck me up as much as she wanted to fuck me. Finally, I went to Sweet Jesus and told him about my situation. He promised to help, and from then on Crazy Mary with the wooden teeth didn't bother me anymore.

She didn't bother anyone. The really scary people like Huey Newton didn't bother me. Huey and I met at a party in Oakland and then did cocaine in my hotel room. As we got high, the Black Panthers' minister of defense got angry because his woman was coming on to me and I didn't tell her to stop.

The scene got very tense. It seemed certain something was going to happen. Either Huey was going to lose control and hurt me or I was going to provoke him into hurting me by saying something stupid. Both seemed likely.

We were talking about jail. He admitted to being worried about going to prison himself.

"Why you scared of jail?" I asked.

"'Cuz if I go, everyone's going to want to fuck me," he said.

I didn't disagree.

"But if they put their dick in my mouth," he added, "I'm gonna bite it off."

"That's a plan," I said. "But right before you bite, you know, you're going to taste that dick in your mouth and wonder whether or not you like it."

Huey Newton shot up from his seat and punched me. The blow caught me on the side of the head.

"Fuck you."

It could've been messy. Both of us were high, we had guns, and we were out of our minds. Fortunately, I decided my best move was to watch as Huey grabbed his woman and marched out of my room.

I knew that I could stir up more shit on stage than in a revolution.

I could be a revolutionary, but I liked white women. I have a white-women disease.

One night when I was snorting cocaine in Haywood's house in Sausalito, I met Casey de la Vega, a stewardess who I referred to as the Contessa for both her beauty and the sound of her last name. She fell in love with my sense of helplessness, treating me as if I was a doll or something. She cooked for me, dressed me, and even tried giving me her Porsche.

A few months later she followed me back to L.A. There was no single reason I left Berkeley and returned home. By the end of 1970

I just felt full. I knew it was time to go back and resume my career as Richard Pryor, comedian.

For the first time in my life, I had a sense of Richard Pryor the person. I understood myself. I knew what I stood for. I knew what I thought. I knew what I had to do.

I had to go back and tell the truth.

The truth.

People can't always handle it.

But I knew that if you tell the truth, it's going to be funny.

PART 2

Mudbone,
part two

FASCINATIN'. THAT'S WHAT HE IS. COURSE THE BOY KNEW NOTHIN'
'bout the shit he was talkin' 'bout, but knowin' shit ain't no prerequisite
for achievin' great things. Lotta stupid people think they're smart and a
lotta smart people know they're stupid. Everybody else, they just workst
hard, try to get by, drink every now and then, and take a little pussy.

Ol' Rich was like that in some respects. He blew back into town too
stupid to know better and too smart to care. The government was about to
get all over his ass for not payin' taxes. Woman sued his ass for child support.
And then his ex-wife was 'bout to get a divorce from him. If he'd taken
the time to think 'bout things, he might not've come back to California.

Told me once, "My wife went to court, man, and she looked so young
and pretty, like a little girl, and I said, 'Who is that bitch?' She told the
judge this and that, and when I looked up, he was crying. The judge was
crying.

"I looked at my lawyer and asked, 'What do I do now?' and he said,
'You're on your own, Rich.'

"Then the judge said, 'Nigger, we want everything. Do you have any
dreams? 'Cuz we want them, too.'"

After the boy finished tellin' me that, I took a taste of wine and
remarked that dreams is the blood of the soul and that he obviously possessed

135

way too much soul for any judge to take away. That's what drugs do to ya. Leech the soul. Course, he didn't listen to me 'bout that, either. Was too busy gettin' that cocaine in his nose. Reminded me of a dog lickin' his balls.

Called him every day for a week and asked, "Boy, whatch you doin'?"

"More," he said.

"Well, you wanna go do somethin' else?"

And each time he said, "Why?"

No one there to tell the motherfucker otherwise.

IT WAS DIFFERENT when I first went to Hollywood. See, after the Big One—World War Two—I tried to get into the motion picture business, too. Read about it in the papers. Said, "We want stars." Shit, in that respect, I was just like Rich. I knowed I was a star. Natural-born. 'Cause I couldn't do nothin' else.

Also, I figured Hollywood was gonna be like it'd been in France. Wall-to-wall pussy.

So I come out and went for this audition. Motherfucker said it was for King Kong. He gave me the script. I didn't know what the story was. King Kong. I said, "I don't mind being a king. Shit, that's a pretty good part. Change the motherfucker's last name, you know, to Williams or somebody. A little too Chinese for me, that Kong shit."

The director said, "I don't believe you understand. What I'm trying to say is that this is a movie about a gorilla."

I replied, "Well, you got the wrong nigger, motherfucker. I ain't no motherfucking gorilla. And I don't appreciate you calling me to this audition."

I took the script and threw the motherfucker down. Them mother-fuckers had me out of there so fast, motherfucking dirt didn't even get on the rug. Snatched me right out like that. And I got on the freight train and went all the way back home.

Here I am at two years and eleven months (1943).

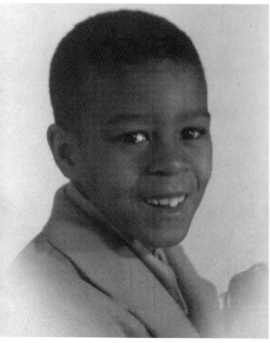

Here I am at eleven (1952).

Mama!

With a friend on board a ship
bound for Germany, where I served
in the Army from 1958 to 1960.

above
Developing my act in the
early 1960s.

right
Early 1970s.

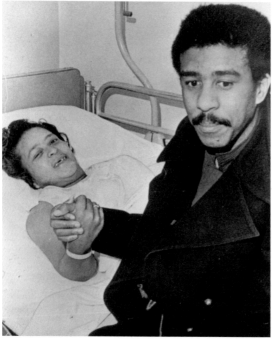

above
Shooting pool with Uncle Dickie,
Aunt Maxine and Pops.

left
With my mother, Gertrude.

right
In concert (mid-1970s).

below
During the filming of *The Bingo Long Traveling All-Stars and Motor Kings* (1976).

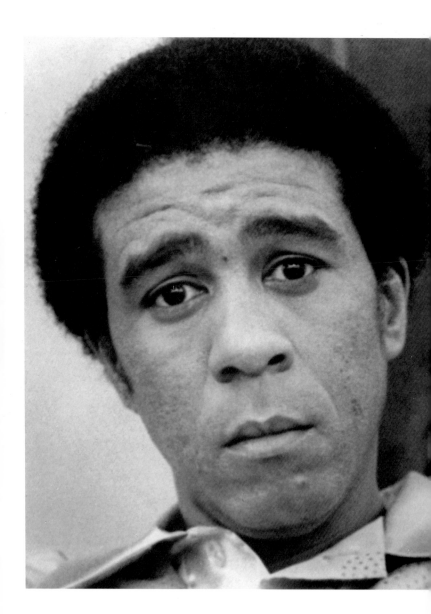
On the set of *Blue Collar* (1977).

above
Which Way Is Up? (1977).

right
Cutting the cake with Jennifer at our
wedding in Hana, Maui, Hawaii (1978).

Relaxing with Jennifer in Hana, Maui, Hawaii (1978).

With my miniature horse, Ginger (1978).

Poolside with Jennifer in Northridge, California (1978).

In the kitchen of our Northridge house with Jennifer and Sammy Davis, Jr. (1979).

Live on the Sunset Strip (1981).

above
Some Kind of Hero (1982).

right
With Paul Mooney in Las Vegas
(1982).

above
With Margaret
Avery, Quincy Jones,
Whoopie Goldberg
and Richard, Jr. on
the set of *The Color
Purple* (1985).

left
With Flynn, wife No.
5 and 6 (1985).

above   With Mitzi Shore, David Letterman and Robin Williams (1989).
below   With Eddie Murphy, Sidney Poitier and Bill Cosby (1989).

My last performance at the Comedy Store (1996).

With Rodney Dangerfield (1996).

Still smokin' (1996).

Surrounded by my children (clockwise from top left): Richard, Jr.; Rain; Elizabeth; Steven; Randis (my grandson); Kelsey; and Franklin (1993).

Considerin' that experience, maybe I should've warned the boy. 'Cause I knew what was gonna happen to him. Could've told him nobody in Hollywood give niggers no good parts. Oh, they'll smile at you, take you out to lunch, let you get some money in your pocket. But they still be lookin' at you like you were a gorilla.

Take what they did to the boy. They pretended to be there for him. Scratching his back. Hollering. "We gotcha, Rich. No worries, brother." 'Cept when he fell, you know what? They missed his skinny black ass.

They caught the monies.

No problems there.

But they missed his ass.

Fortunately, the boy's like one of them old-time niggers. In them days, niggers were too hungry to die. Nowadays, you shoot a nigger, he falls over. And sad to say, most of the niggers nowadays be shootin' themselves. Doin' the dirty work themselves. Shit. Ain't got no pride. Back in the old days, nigger'd live just to spite the motherfucker who wanted him dead. Didn't want to give up the wine or the pussy.

That's what Rich was like. Didn't want to give none of it up. In fact, he wanted more. More, more, more.

"Did you ever get it?" I asked.

"That's the thing about being an addict," he said. "You never know. Good or bad, you never know."

18

BACK IN L.A., I STARTED WORKING OUT AGAIN AT REDD FOXX'S club. One night Redd gave me a fedora to wear. It was more than a friendly gesture. I saw it as the passing of a torch. The master had given me his blessing.

I took it seriously. My first concert film, *Smokin'*, filmed at the Improv in New York, in April 1971, contained new bits like "Black Cat with Neat Hair," "Colored Guys Have Big Ones," and "Dracula and the Brother." My second album, *Craps After Hours*, also explored race, sex, and drugs, but with even more shape and sting.

I knew routines dealing with getting high, fucking my wife's girlfriend, and rednecks looking for pussy were different from anyone else's. But I didn't want merely to shock people. I also wanted to be good. I wanted my stand-up to be like a night at the theater.

Mooney was the one who told me what people thought about me. I was hot in the black community long before I cracked the mainstream. But word spread. Clubs were packed whenever I played. My shows were events, sojourns into territory considered dangerous, taboo, and, as all of us know, true to life.

That's part of what made it so damn exciting. Me and the audience were breaking new ground.

People don't talk about nothing real. Like you talk about shit that's real. Like jackin' off.

A lot of people say they don't jack off.

I did.

I used to jack off so much I knew pussy couldn't be as good as my hand.

I didn't see why that shit I talked about was considered controversial. It didn't make sense.

You can't talk about fucking in America. People say you're dirty. But if you talk about killing somebody, that's cool.

My personal life had no brilliances either. I lived with Casey in a house overlooking the Sunset Strip. It was not a scene that could be described as loving or tranquil.

We had a birthday party at a fancy restaurant once. Invited a lot of people. Got dressed up.

But Casey and I arrived fighting and continued yelling through dinner. Finally, the waiter served the cake. I blew out the candles and then smashed the cake in Casey's face.

As I got up to leave, the waiter offered her a towel. In a deliberate, ladylike fashion, she cleaned herself up and then to the waiter said, "I'll have my coffee now."

That was tame compared to the other shenanigans that went on when the Contessa wasn't around. Sometimes I spent days at a time hanging out, snorting cocaine, and bullshitting with Mooney (the only one who never got high), Dirty Dick, and Prophet, an artist friend who resembled Miles Davis. When the air cleared, we ventured down the hill to the Candy Store or the Daisy, exclusive private clubs in Beverly Hills.

I wasn't a star, but they still let us rub elbows with a crowd that included Elizabeth Taylor, Peter Lawford, and Sal Mineo. Once, I saw a drunk Richard Harris chase Bobby Darin out of the Daisy. At the Candy Store, I followed Kim Novak around like a dog hoping for a sniff. Another time, Mooney and I arrived just as Steve McQueen was leaving. He shoved his face straight into mine and asked, "Is that Dick Pryor? Is that him?" I looked him right back and said, "No."

As I walked by, I heard him say to Mooney, "The guy looks just like him."

"And you look just like Steve McQueen," Mooney said.

If that was a put-on, I was once the victim of an even better act than mine. I spotted her standing beside the dance floor at the Candy Store. She told me her name was Mitrasha, and she was as beautiful and exotic as her name, a dead ringer for Josephine Baker. After a night of drinking, flirting, kissing, and dancing, I took Mitrasha home, where we did blow and got down to business.

The next time we were together, Mitrasha forgot to do the tuck and fold. When I reached down, I discovered that she was actually a he. For some reason, I didn't care. Either I wanted the nut too badly, I was too high to object, or I was as sexually confused as Mitrasha. It was probably a combination of all three reasons.

Mitrasha and I carried on for several weeks. We even went out dancing at the Daisy. I never kept him a secret. Mooney, for instance, knew I was fucking a dude, and a drop-dead gorgeous one at that. I even admitted doing something different was exciting. But after two weeks of being gay, enough was enough and I went back to life as a horny heterosexual.

I was the only dude in the neighborhood who'd fuck this faggot. A lot of dudes won't play that shit.

In the daytime.

But at night, they be knockin' on the door.

Then I saw him like ten years later. He be, "Hi, Rich."

A while later Mooney delivered a message from Mitrasha. He'd realized a lifelong dream and undergone a sex-change operation. Now biologically a woman, she wanted to get back together.

I passed.

By then, I had more than enough to handle.

Given the word on the street, I wasn't surprised Motown founder Berry Gordy and director Sidney Furie assumed a lot of shit about me when I auditioned for *Lady Sings the Blues*. From the questions they asked, I realized they thought I was a junkie. They thought I shot up heroin. I never had.

But if it was going to get me a job, I didn't mind, you know.

"What would you say to Billie Holliday if you caught her doing drugs?" asked Sidney.

I closed my eyes for a moment. I'd grown up around people like Billie Holliday. I knew women like her. I knew that if I was her friend and caught her doing drugs, I wouldn't be surprised. I wouldn't get angry. I might not like it, but I'd understand, I'd be sympathetic to her need.

So I pretended to fix up some shit as I talked to her. Said, "Baby, how could you be doin', you know... Don't be thinkin' you're hidin' it..."

They gave me the role of Piano Man right there. They said I did great.

I was very excited. I talked about becoming a movie star all the time. Not because I saw myself as a star. I just had all this juice inside me, this swirl of emotions and ideas that I felt could be brought out on the big screen.

"You're the greatest actor I ever seen," Mooney once said. "You know why? Cause you can't act."

"I can't?"

"No, but you sure can lie. You convince yourself of somethin' and then you tell it like it was true."

And so it was in *Lady Sings the Blues*. I modeled myself after a piano player I knew from Collins' Corner in Peoria, named Jimmy Brinkley, and I tried not to get high as we shot the movie. It seemed to let me hold my own. Diana Ross was great, mysterious, gorgeous. Billy Dee's self-assurance in front of the camera made me jealous, though I thought he took himself way too seriously. At the end, I felt like I'd opened a new door.

Suddenly, people wanted to meet me. One night Warren Beatty and Julie Christie came to my place. We talked about movies and sheep. Julie owned sheep in England; Warren wanted me to do a movie with him. But I worried that if we worked together I wouldn't like him as much.

I accepted another offer instead. Mel Brooks called and asked if I was interested in working with him on a script for a western. Mel and I had never met, but I knew of his brilliant reputation starting with Sid Caesar. I was excited just to talk to him. After the script arrived, I read it quickly, and Mel and I talked again.

"So this is a comedy?" I asked.

"Yes," he said.

"Then why don't you make it one?"

I joined Mel in New York, where he set up shop in a hotel with writers Andrew Bergman, Norman Steinberg, and Alan Unger. We tossed out lines and acted out ideas each day for eight or nine hours. Mel acted as ringleader, saying stuff like, "Great, Richard, we'll make this guy black," and laughing when I came up with the fart scene.

I knew *Blazing Saddles* was going to be one of the funniest scripts ever, and before we even finished writing it Mel was talking about me starring as the black sheriff. But when it came time to make the movie, I think people at the studio more powerful than Mel didn't want me.

They were scared of my reputation. Yes, I was funny, nobody could deny that. But they also saw me as a volatile, vulgar, profane black man who wisecracked about getting high and screwing white women. It scared the shit out of their Brooks Brothers sensibilities to think about risking millions of dollars on a movie starring a person like me.

I think Mel liked me, and I think he could've fought to keep me as his star. I think Cleavon Little did a good job. However, I know what kind of job I could've done. But Mel, bless his heart, had a decision to make, and he chose to get his movie made.

It might've been different had *Lady Sings the Blues* come out before *Blazing Saddles*. The reviews I got for playing Piano Man surely would've changed some of those tight-assed minds. But both films were shot at the same time.

Some ten years later I saw Mel in a bathroom at a nightclub in London and he tried to make amends.

"If it wasn't for you, I wouldn't have been able to do it," he said.

"Don't tell me that here," I said. "Tell them that on television."

And then we both laughed.

Carefully.

Following the release of *Lady Sings the Blues*, I should've been one of the hottest young actors in Hollywood. There was talk of an Oscar nomination in the press. People knew that I'd cowritten *Blazing Saddles*, one of the funniest pictures ever. I had ideas and talent. I deserved the type of multipicture deal that filmmakers Spike Lee and Robert Townsend would get from studios fifteen years later.

But that wasn't happening then. The only scripts that came my way were for low-budget, exploitation films. It was as if baseball player Barry Bonds had a great season and then was forced to begin the next one in the minors.

Still, I took what was available, including *Wattstax*, *Hit*, and *The Mack*.

It was frustrating not to be able to do serious work. I felt shackled, teased, and tortured by the system. But what were the options?

I went to see Logan's Run, *right. They had a movie of the future called* Logan's Run. *There ain't no niggers in it.*

I said, "Well, white folks ain't planning for us to be here. That's why we got to make movies. But we got to make some really hip movies. Not movies about pimps. We done made enough movies about pimps, because white folks already know about pimping. 'Cuz we the biggest whores they got."

I couldn't win. In 1973 I worked on the picture *Some Call It Loving*, which shot for several days at a church in South Central L.A. One afternoon the priest invited me into his office. An elderly black man sat in the corner. The priest, oblivious to the onlooker, informed me in a grave tone of voice that several girls who'd been watching the production claimed that I'd molested them. I was as high as a bubble band, but I still knew bullshit when I heard it.

"That's what they claim?" I asked.

"Yes," he said.

"Well, they're wrong," I snapped. "I didn't molest them. I fucked them. And their dogs, too."

Suddenly, the old black man perked up. As I stormed out, he asked me why I'd said that.

"They're talking bullshit," I said. "So I just added to it."

19

IN 1973 TELEVISION, NORMALLY THE MOST RESTRICTIVE MEDIUM, turned into an unanticipated land of opportunity. Flip Wilson and Lily Tomlin were launching shows. As a rule, variety shows were as unhip as vanilla ice cream. But Flip and Lily wanted their shows to have an edge, and they saw me as the guy who could add that exotic spice.

For me, Flip's show was an opportunity to delve further into characters that I was developing in my stage act. During one sketch, Redd Foxx and I played a couple hustlers in a pool hall that reminded me of Pop's place in Peoria. Before he taped, Redd gave me an old overcoat that helped me get into character, but I did so good that he took the coat back as soon as we finished.

"Why do you want it back?" I asked.

"Because you were funny," he said.

"Do you like the coat?"

"I do now," he replied.

"Shit."

I was more inspired while working on Lily's two specials later that year. That was no doubt due to the way I felt about Lily herself. She turned me on. I went gaga over the way she dressed up in various outfits and became all those different people. I thought she was phenomenal and loved watching her work. She'd make me goofus from laughing so hard.

Then she'd switch gears and inject a poignancy that made you think about the way you looked at the world. That shit was inspiring. It took comedy to a different level. I tried doing the same during a skit in which I played a junkie in a soul-food café, someone hoping to get both dignity and dinner. In another bit, Lily and I were a prejudiced aristocrat and a smelly wino who bridged their differences while stuck in an elevator.

"I may be a wino," my character, Lightnin' Bug Johnson, stated. "But I'm still a gentleman."

"Goodbye, Mr. Johnson," her Miss Audrey Earbore said. "Stay in touch."

Lily and I went to each other's house a few times. She was always inspiring. We got each other. We had conversations that spiraled into the ozone. In minutes, we'd create enough characters to populate entire neighborhoods. And the deeper and funnier it got, the more I wanted to get into her pants. But nothing ever happened, and we stayed friends and admirers.

The following year, Lily's second special won an Emmy award for comedy writing. I gave mine to Miss Whittaker and the Carver Center. If not for her, I never would've gotten that award.

If not for her, I never would've gotten anywhere.

Not that everything was hunky-dory. In 1974, after *Blazing Saddles* finally reached theaters, my ignorance of the law, rejection of society's rules, and general lack of responsibility caught up with me. First, I was stopped by cops one night for outstanding traffic warrants while driving Mooney's 1952 Ford and, as was my custom, I didn't have any ID on me.

It wasn't a pretty picture as I tried to assure the police officer I was who I said I was.

He prefer to throw my ass in jail.

Cops put a hurtin' on your ass, man. They really degrade you. White folks don't believe that shit. They don't believe cops degrade you.

"Oh, come on, those beatings," white folk say. "Those people were resisting arrest."

That's 'cuz the police live in your neighborhood. Niggers don't know 'em like that. See, white folks get a ticket, they pull over. "Hey, officer, glad to be of help."

Nigger got to be talking about, "I—am—reaching—into—my—pocket—for—my—license!" You know? 'Cuz I don't want to be no motherfucking accident.

As soon as that was cleaned up, the government kicked my ass by filing an indictment for failure to pay income taxes on $250,000 earned between 1967 and 1970. It looked to me like *The People v. Richard Pryor*, otherwise known as *David and Goliath, Part II: Screw the Nigger*.

I tried to explain, but "Oops" didn't cover it.

Neither did "Sorry" or "I'll try harder next year."

My lawyers plea-bargained four counts against me down to a $2,500 fine and ten days in jail.

I went to jail for income tax evasion. I didn't know a motherfucking thing about no taxes. I told the judge, "Your Honor, I forgot."

He said, "You'll remember next year, nigger."

With the release of my third album, *That Nigger's Crazy*, I hit the road. This was breakthrough time. The LP sold more than 1 million copies and became my first crossover success. I wish I had a dollar for every person who's told me how they hid that album from their parents and laughed all night when they finally dared to play it.

But that's cool. That's how it was supposed to be.

This was new stuff. It was like listening to Lenny.

Everything was fair game. There was no turning back.

I had found my groove.

◆   ◆   ◆

Not everyone approved. My grandmother told me not to use her anymore on records. Told me she didn't talk like that. I said, "Mama, you forgot."

Others couldn't help themselves. Backstage in Detroit, two black cops told me that they'd arrested a black guy who started spouting my line, "I—am—reaching—into—my—pocket." They nailed him for doing Richard Pryor and then finished the routine, saying, "Okay, spread them cheeks. Put your face on the ground." Then all of them laughed.

That was beautiful.

In Hollywood, I didn't have to say nothing to be popular. I walked into the Daisy one night and its owner, Jack Hansen, skewered me with his arm and proclaimed with a broad grin, "Richard, you're a movie star. Now we can fuck!" But that's how it went. I waved at women and they were mine.

If that was a joke, Deboragh McGuire, an exquisite black model in her early twenties, didn't get it. After spotting her on a few occasions at the Candy Store, she ignored my pantomimed pickup attempts without so much as a smile or a wink in return. Nothing. Which made me want her even more. Each time I turned to my companions, usually Mooney or my friend David Banks, and whined how badly I wanted to leave with her.

I wanted it so badly it hurt. Truly hurt.

Finally, one Friday night David said, "Man, it might help your case if you talked to her."

"Why don't you do it for me?" I asked.

David, who's the definition of jive, squiggled up his face.

"I don't got nothin' to say to her."

"Don't fuck with me," I said. "Go over there and tell her I want to talk to her."

That was a mistake. It was like asking Don King to be brief. David was overkill. She didn't like him. However, in order to get him away from the table, Debbie offered to compromise.

"If he gets up off his ass," she said, "then maybe I'll talk to him."

After sending over a bottle of champagne, I walked over and let her talk to me like a dog. But I liked it, you know? Reluctantly, she agreed to drive with me back to my house for a party. I'd invited Lola Falana and some other friends. Later, Debbie confessed the only reason she had gone was to meet *Soul Train*'s host Don Cornelius.

Even though I was bedeviled by her, Deboragh didn't like me. She didn't need me. As a teenager, she had met this rich, older white man who helped her skip through the massacre. He taught her things, took her places, and she loved him.

That fact alone made me insanely jealous. I telephoned Debbie as if hers was the only number I knew. Day and night. The more attached she was to him, the more determined I was to take her away. It was sick, really it was.

I tried to get Debbie to hang out with me on the set of *Uptown Saturday Night*, but she wasn't ready to get involved with my craziness.

I didn't blame her. One night I got so pissed at not being paid nearly $100,000 in royalties owed me for *That Nigger's Crazy*, I opened fire on my gold album—not to mention the wall—with a .345 Magnum. Another night Freddie Prinze and I, after getting nuts on coke, stood in the backyard and fired round after round into the sky.

The Contessa, who was still living with me, freaked out. She felt as if World War Three was breaking out in the Hollywood Hills. She called Mooney and asked him to come over and calm us down.

"He won't stop doing coke!" she wailed. "He's crazy!"

You can't tell nobody not to snort no cocaine. Motherfucker's gonna snort it anyway. It took me a long time to learn that shit'll kill you. Once a big booger came out of my nose. A motherfucking black one this long. Scared the shit out of me. I said, "Goddamn, please, I'll quit. Just let it stop."

The only thing that stopped was me and Casey. One night in early 1975, we went to a party up in the Hollywood Hills. Without telling me, Casey left with a friend of mine who had become a well-known actor. They got into my car, which was parked alongside the curb, and began some kind of funny business driving lesson.

Before long, we heard a loud crash. Everybody left the party and ran outside. The neighborhood was quiet and dark. However, we didn't have to look hard to see the source of all the noise. My car had crashed through the house down the hill. The tail end was sticking out. It looked like a stunt from a movie.

Casey and my friend were okay, but neither offered an explanation. But Mooney offered a guess:

"He must've been teaching her how to use a stick shift," he said.

It didn't matter to me.

I bought a new car, and Casey packed up her shit and made plans to get the hell out.

I don't mind women leaving me, see. But they tell you why. Fuck that. Just leave. You know? 'Cuz there ain't shit you can say while they're talking to you. 'Cuz you know it's true. All you can do is stand there and look silly.

But when the shit gets too thick, nigger's got a great answer.

"Well, fuck it then! Take your shit and get out. Yeah, motherfucker. Pack this. You packing shit. Pack this motherfucking shit. Goddamn it. I don't care where you put this shit. I don't give a fuck where you put this shit. Shit, I'm gonna find me some new pussy."

She didn't give a shit what I did or said. Somehow she made everything seem like my fault.

Women come back at your ass, though, "If you had two more inches of dick, you'd find some new pussy here."

Bullshit.

"I know the dick was good to ya. If it wasn't good, why was you hollerin'?"

"I was hollerin' to keep from laughing in your face."

Nothing was as terrifying as rejection.
Even when it worked for you.

20

BY EARLY 1975, I WAS A HOT COMMODITY, AND IF I WANTED to grab a lucrative payday, one was there for the taking. TV series. Las Vegas casinos. Millions of dollars. But the money didn't interest me. I knew that if I was any good, it was going to be there regardless.

Instead, I went the opposite direction. Declined everything and continued pursuing my own thing. My manager at the time didn't understand. He knew the futility of asking me to tone down the shit I did on stage. But he pleaded with me to think sensibly. He wanted those monies.

"What I'm saying might be profane," I explained. "But it's also profound."

My belief in myself was unwavering. My job, as I saw it, was to throw light where there had been only darkness. I was John Wayne, taking up the fight for freedom and justice. Then Roberta Flack introduced me to Atlanta-based attorney, David Franklin, the only black manager I knew of in the business, and I felt as if I'd found the guy who could help me become the hero I envisioned.

We couldn't have been more dissimilar. David was straight, upright, and uptight. I was a mess, short-fused, paranoid, unpredictable.

However, we had a common interest—respect. Both of us wanted it. For ourselves and other people.

We were going to break down all the barriers.

As teammates.

He'd block, I'd head toward the goal line.

The roll began during a five-week run at the Comedy Store—my gymnasium—where I began preparing new material for another album. One night between bits, I saw the likeness of an old man I'd seen somewhere else. Somewhere in my life, you know? It was as if he was standing beside me onstage. Right there, waiting for me to notice.

"Over here, Rich. Look at me."

Once I noticed him, inspiration took over. As with other characters I did, like the wino or Oilwell, I suddenly knew everything about this wise old man who I called Mudbone. Every black town had someone like him. Some old geezer who talked shit about his life's experiences. Fancied himself a philosopher. That first night I talked about Mudbone for two minutes. A month later I did a half hour on him alone.

I didn't know if he was any good as a character. But I liked him as a person.

I imagined myself at that age.

I was born in Peoria, Illinois—that's a city, nigger. And when I was little, there was an old man. His name was Mudbone. And he dipped snuff. And he'd sit in front of the barbecue pit and he'd spit. See, that was his job.

I'm pretty sure that was his job, because that's all he did. But he'd tell fascinatin' stories…

My third album, *Is It Something I Said?*, was recorded over a week of performances at the Latin Casino in Cherry Hill, New Jersey.

The O'Jays opened the show. I'd never seen them. I stood backstage and listened. They were fantastic. The place was nuts. Then it was my turn and no one would settle down.

"Please take your seats," the emcee said over and over.

But no one listened.

Finally, I walked out, grabbed the mike, and said, "Will you niggers please sit down!"

And they did.

Then I went on and did a show that stands out as one of my best ever.

Good God, there are a whole lot of niggers here today. And some white folks too. You motherfuckers came in a bunch, didn't you! . . . Shortage of white folks lately. You all stop fucking? White folks into yoga. You can't get no nut doing yoga. You have to get the pus–say!

They stop fucking because some white man told them there were too many people on Earth. There's no room for him to ride his horsey.

There will be no shortage of niggers. Niggers are fucking.

We got to have somebody here to take over!

The comedy gods have many tentacles, you know. And they swoop down and touch you at different times. But when they do it's like salvation. Or deliverance. It's as close to flying as man gets.

The magic doesn't happen often, but when you're on and rolling nothing that I've ever touched comes close.

Not cocaine.

Not pussy.

Afterward, David Banks went back to L.A. to edit the tapes, while I traveled to New York to host "Saturday Night Live." In only its first few weeks, the show had emerged like a gunshot blast as the hottest, hippest show on TV.

Even though "SNL"'s cast members John Belushi, Chevy Chase, and Dan Aykroyd pushed the envelope each weekend, the show's producers were concerned that I might take it too far even for them. During rehearsals, writer Michael O'Donoghue came to my hotel room to discuss ideas, but my suggestions scared the hell out of him, and all he could say was, "You can't do that on television."

"See, that's what I'm talking about!" I protested, airing my frustration over the constraints of TV.

Aside from that, I never heard any discussion of censorship. No talk about holding back from anyone, including the cast, who gave me the impression that they didn't listen to shit anyway. Behind the scenes, though, the network wrung their hands over the possibility that I might say "fuck," and producer Lorne Michaels, bowing to that concern, secretly installed a five-second delay to the live broadcast, giving NBC a chance to bleep it.

If I'd known, I never would've shown up.

In any event, I caught the cast's enthusiasm, and I think it was reflected in the show. Following an opening monologue—my *Exorcist* routine from *That Nigger's Crazy*—Belushi and I traded swipes as samurai bellboys who argued about which one of us got to carry a guest's luggage upstairs. It ended when I took my sword and cut the front desk in half, prompting Belushi—in the only sentence he'd ever utter in English as that character—to say, "I can see where you're coming from."

But we really stretched the rubber band of what was normally seen on television in a skit where Chevy Chase was a personnel executive giving me a job interview. Although our "word association" game began innocuously with words like "dog" and "tree," the game quickly escalated to a tension-filled contest of racial epithets when Chevy said, "White."

"Black," I replied.

"Bean," he said.

"Pod," I responded.

"Negro.

"Whitie."

"Tarbaby."

"What'd you say?"

"Tarbaby."

"Ofay."

"Colored."

"Redneck."

"Jungle bunny."

"Peckerwood."

"Burrhead."

"Cracker."

"Spear-chucker."

"White trash."

"Jungle bunny."

"Honkey."

"Spade."

"Honkey-honkey."

"Nigger!"

"Deeeeeead honkey!"

Movies were next. Although *The Bingo Long Traveling All-Stars and Motor Kings*, *Car Wash*, and *Silver Streak* were all box office winners, each one had its disappointments. I wasn't speaking to Billy Dee when we did *Bingo Long*. On the set of *Car Wash*, I was too coked out to know any better. And after *Silver Streak*, which began as a minor part but ended as a co-starring role with Gene Wilder, I felt I could have done better.

Afterward, I was inundated with scripts, but I worried that my insurgent brand of humor didn't translate as well to the silver screen as I'd hoped. Although my funky, jive-talking characterizations gave credibility to otherwise poorly written cutouts, I still felt limited by the ideas other people had originally created.

And in that way I compromised what I wanted to stand for.

But then maybe I was just fooling myself by thinking there was more freedom in movies, since I was never going to find an outlet as unrestricted as the stage. Just me, the mike, and the audience.

You knew that, Rich.

Yes, I did.

So?

Well, there was still a little child inside me who wanted to go behind the screen as I'd done in Peoria and look for Little Beaver.

And?

The monies. I wanted the monies.

So what'd you expect?

More than I got.

You all know how black humor started? It started on slave ships. Cat was rowing and dude says, "What you laughin' about?"

He said, "Yesterday I was a king."

Deboragh and I went fishing in Hawaii. Since I was a child, I've loved to fish. We always argued about who was *going* to catch the biggest fish, and at the end of the day, we argued about who *had* caught the biggest fish. However, on this particular day, we were out in deep water when she caught a motherfucker that had no intention of letting her pull him in. But she put up a fight that matched his and got him all the way up to the boat.

I took one look at the motherfucker and worried that he was going to get on board and say, "You caught the wrong fish, motherfuckers. Now everyone in the water. Let's see who filets who."

You know?

But this fish took a turn and then jumped straight up into the air. Broke Deboragh's line. You could hear it go.

Ping!

We looked at each other and laughed. We'd had so much fun. We had fun just thinking about it later on. Hemingway wrote one of my favorite books about a monster fish that got away. On *Bicentennial Nigger*, my fourth and most political album, I tried explaining that sometimes the shit you don't get is as memorable as the shit you do get, you know.

They'll have some nigger two hundred years old in blackface. Stars and stripes on his forehead. Little eyes and lips just jiving. And he'll have that lovely white-folks expression on his face. But he's happy. He's happy cause he'd been here two hundred years.

He'll say, "I'm just so thrilled to be here. Over here in America. I'm so glad you all took me out of my home. I used to live to be a hundred fifty. Now I die of high blood pressure by the time I'm fifty-two. That thrills me to death. I'm just so pleased America's going to last.

"They brought me over here in a boat. There was four hundred of us come over here. Three hundred sixty of us died on the way over here. I love that. That just thrills me so.

"I don't know, you white folks are so good to us. Got over here and another twenty of us died from disease. Ah, but you didn't have no doctors to take care of us. I'm so sorry you didn't. Upset y'all, too, didn't it?

"Then you split us all up, yes, sir. Took my mama over that way. My wife went that way. Took my kids over yonder. I'm just so happy. I don't know what to do. I don't know what to do if I get two hundred more years of this.

"Lordy, mercy. I don't know where my own mama is now. She up yonder, in that big white boat in the sky.

"Y'all probably done forgot about it. But I ain't gonna never forget."

21

WOMEN. DRUGS. MOVIES.

It doesn't matter. One of the scariest things in life is to get what you wish for.

Toward the end of 1976 producer Hannah Weinstein asked me to go through the script for *Greased Lightning*, a film based on the life of black stock-car driver Wendell Scott. As I sat on her living-room floor, she ticked off the film's different characters as well as the actors she had in mind to play them, including Cleavon Little. I heard his name and assumed he was going to play Scott.

"Who do you want me to play?" I asked.

She looked at me as if I was stupid.

"The lead," she said. "You're going to play Wendell Scott."

Well, that fucked me up. Although I complained that the only reason I made stupid films like *Car Wash* and *Silver Streak* was because they were the only scripts offered, I was blown away when a movie that seemed to have substance came along and the producers wanted me to star. Was I ready to carry a film?

Said you were, motherfucker.

Yes, but…

*I was going to be cool for about four weeks (back when I was a kid),
hanging with my man Matt. Matt was bad. Knockin' motherfuckers out.
Bam! Bam! He was a killer, Jack.*

*Henry Hanson, though, he'd knock a motherfucker through a brick
wall. Matt backed off. Then I was standing there all alone. Henry say,
"What you got to do with it, little nigger?"*

*"I was just—I come home with Matt. I wasn't doing nothin'. I was
gonna play some basketball. Can I go now?"*

The movie was shot in Madison, Georgia. It got off to a rocky
start when the original director, Melvin Van Peebles, tried stirring up
shit about there not being enough jobs for blacks on the production.
His effort fizzled when I refused to support him.

I said, "Man, I got a job. What the fuck are you talking
about?" He was replaced by Michael Schultz, who'd directed *Car
Wash.*

It was a nod toward keeping me in line. Though I hadn't been
involved, the studio worried about my volatile reputation. I was more
concerned about doing a good job, and to that end I vowed to stay
clean throughout the entire movie. I rented a farmhouse on some of
the prettiest property I'd ever seen, and flew my grandmother out
from Peoria to take care of things.

Through thick and thin, Mama was like a security blanket for
me. She knew the real Richard Pryor. There was no need to pretend
around her. I don't know how she felt about hanging around a movie
set, but she liked fishing, and we spent a lot of time together casting
our lines in a beautiful freshwater lake out in the field. One day she
caught the biggest bass of her life. Started to scream as if she
wanted to tell Jesus himself.

That was nice, Mama, wasn't it?

Meantime, I hooked my co-star, Pam Grier. The first scene we shot was a romantic one with both of us in the bathtub. I tried to be truly amazing. The director yelled "Action." Pam sang "Amazing Grace" in my ear. It was quite a scene.

Pam and I stayed together for about six months. After the movie, we went on a romantic getaway to Barbados, where she got deathly ill after eating shellfish. Back home, we enjoyed a much healthier life. We shopped, played tennis, watched TV, and hung out.

Unfortunately, our relationship wasn't able to survive Hollywood. Of the two of us, I became the star, but I was put off by how much I thought Pam believed the stardom belonged to her. In my head there was only one Numero Uno, and it wasn't her.

White women take more shit. You be home and shit and you be ready to go out. You say, "I'm going out, baby. Take it easy."

She say, "Okay toodle-loo."

You say that to a black woman, the bitch starts dressing, too. Says, "Yeah, nigger, me too. Shit. What the fuck. You can't go out without me."

After *Greased Lightning*, the pieces fell together. Everyone in town wanted to be in business with me. David Franklin negotiated separate multimillion-dollar deals with Warner Brother and Universal, where I set up offices in a bungalow next door to Telly Savalas. I also had projects going with Paramount and Columbia.

As befitted my new stature, I spent $500,000 on a Spanish-style hacienda on three and a half acres in Northridge, a rural suburb outside of L.A. An electronic gate kept unwanted visitors out, while its guesthouse, tennis court, pool, orange groves, and a stable—home to a miniature pony—made it seem as if I never had to leave.

On the downside, the estate was in utter disrepair inside and out. The rambling grounds were overgrown and forlorn. The interior was shabby and old. In a way, the house was very much like me. It looked good. It had tremendous possibilities. But it needed work.

I got some money and finally bought a house. First house I ever had. And them motherfuckers who come to fix it, boy, they can kill you. Everything's five hundred dollars when they come to your house.

"What do you want? It's five hundred dollars."

I said, "I ain't told you what I want."

"I don't give a fuck. It's five hundred dollars."

I hired Lucy Saroyan, the daughter of writer William Saroyan and Carol Matthau (she'd remarried Walter Matthau), to redecorate from top to bottom. Some blonde actress introduced us. Lucy was smart, energetic, and friendly with everybody in Hollywood. She played with life as if it was a toy. I think she thought working for me was going to be a continuation of the party.

But by the time I finished *Which Way Is Up?* in February, Pam and I were sailing on rocky seas. I was pursuing Deboragh again, obsessed with prying her from her older lover. And then I started up with Lucy.

One time when my grandmother was visiting, all three women came by to see her at the same time. They sat in the den, talking as if they were friends. Pam, Debbie, and Lucy. Unable to deal with this, I hid in the bedroom and listened to them make small talk.

Finally, I called my grandmother in to see how things were going.

"Mama, which one of them should I marry?" I asked.

She looked at me as if I'd lost my mind.

"I wouldn't give a nickel for any of those bitches," she said.

My grandmother refused to see me as anything but the little boy she helped raise. That same visit she tossed the housekeeper Mercy and the cook and their helpers out of the kitchen and made dinner. Afterward, she washed dishes and then called me over to help dry. I shook my head as if she'd told a joke. I was watching TV.

"Mama," I laughed.

"You didn't get too big for that, did you?" she asked.

"Mama, I don't want you doing that. I got ladies who do that stuff for me. I pay four people, you know?"

"Does that mean you ain't gonna help?"

A moment later, she stood over me, and I swear to God I never saw the skillet that was in her hand. But I felt it, that's for damn sure. She whacked me good, right over my head like in one of those cartoons. I might as well have been nine years old as she grabbed my collar and led me into the kitchen. I dried everything too—dishes, counters, floors, chairs, tears.

The press said many things about me being the new black superstar; only one thing was certain: it wasn't easy being Richard Pryor. After the movie *Blue Collar*, which Paul Schrader wrote in about two days especially for me and Harvey Keitel, I went straight into preproduction on my own weekly comedy-variety series on NBC.

When I committed to do a ten-week comedy-variety series, I thought I could do something significant. I saw only the possibilities of TV as a way of communicating. I mean, one week of truth on TV would blow people's minds. You got 20 to 50 million people listening to the real shit every week, there's going to be a revolution in the way everybody thinks.

But the reality of what the network censors allowed on prime time undercut all my enthusiasm. Because I didn't want to sell out completely, I walked into one of the earliest meetings with the show's writers—headed up by Mooney and David Banks—and quit the show. I had no heart for the censors, I explained.

"You want to see me with my brains blown out?" I ranted. "I'm gonna have to be ruthless here because of what it does to my life. I'm not stable enough."

I wasn't stable, but it had nothing to do with the censors. In August, Lucy hired her friend Jennifer Lee to assist her while decorating my house. Jennifer was a dark-haired flower who blossomed right in front of my eyes one night as she sat on the edge of a bed and played the guitar and sang.

I encouraged her to hang out more often. She had depth and intelligence. She seemed to understand me more profoundly than anyone I'd ever met. I'd catch her watching me, our eyes would lock, and I knew that she knew the shit I was thinking.

She was in the guest room the night Lucy and I broke up following a deranged night of cocaine and violence. The next morning, Lucy tried to persuade Jenny to leave, too—which would've fucked me over since my house was completely torn apart—but something possessed Jenny to stay. Maybe she knew the trouble had been coke-related. Maybe she wanted me. Maybe she thought she could help me. Or maybe she simply felt safe in the morning light.

In any event, I realized that she could handle herself when our first date—an Andrew Young fund-raiser at the Beverly Wilshire Hotel—ended in potential disaster. We'd gone with a friend and his girlfriend. In the limo on the way back, the girlfriend laid into Jenny about being white and dating a black man.

Sisters look at you like you killed your mama when you're out with a white woman. Why should you be happy?

Outside the door to Jenny's quaint bungalow in West Hollywood, I took her hand and gave her a gentle kiss.

"I'm sorry for what she said in the car," I said. "I don't know what you've heard or read about me. But I don't see colors. I don't believe in prejudice. We're all people, you know? That's hard enough."

And that's the truth.

22

IT WAS WEAKNESS. THE DAY AFTER A PLANE FLEW OVER MY HOUSE towing a sign that said SURRENDER RICHARD, I let myself be swayed into going ahead with the TV series, though I got NBC to agree to reduce the number of shows from ten to four. The less the better.

I should have just taped my personal life and sold it as a weekly drama. Episode one: Although Richard is in love with Jennifer, he proposes to Deboragh.

"I thought Pam Grier said she was marrying you," Deboragh said.

"She did," I replied. "But that's not true. Don't worry about it."

I still don't know whether I wanted to marry Debbie because I loved her or because I figured it was the only way to bring my obsession with her to the point of do or die.

"Well, I first have to talk to *him*," she said, referring to the older man who'd virtually raised her.

"Okay," I said, putting the phone down.

I sounded like a reasonable man. But I wasn't close.

After hanging up, I numbed myself with vodka and cocaine. The demons began hammering my brain. Putting in overtime. Before I knew it, I drove to Deboragh's house and was pounding on her door. No one answered. I screamed.

Suddenly, it opened just a crack—enough for her to look out and tell me that she wasn't going to let me in.

"I'll call you," she promised.

A few days later, she did.

"Okay," she said.

"Okay, what?"

"Okay, you win. I'll marry you."

Episode two: On September 18, Lily Tomlin invited me to appear at a star-studded gay rights benefit at the Hollywood Bowl. By the time I walked on stage, I was out of control. I was drunk, stoned, and incensed at what I perceived to be the mistreatment of a black singing group compared to some of the white acts on the bill. When I got to the mike, I asked 17,000 of the richest, most powerful and influential motherfuckers in Hollywood where they were when Watts burned.

Then I added, "You Hollywood faggots can kiss my rich, happy, black ass."

I was the talk of Hollywood the next day. I'd pissed off everyone from studio heads to headwaiters. Lily tried excusing my behavior, or at least explaining it by saying, "When you hire Richard Pryor, you get Richard."

In the aftermath, I was sorry and ashamed. I regretted the incident. But when you're fucked up and try to make a point, something gets screwed up as the words travel between your brain and mouth.

Your brain says, "You want to say something, Rich? Great. But first come on into the lion's den."

"Oh, okay."

So then you want to tell your wife that you love her, but you end up saying, "Hey, bitch, get off my back."

Episode three: The night before Richard marries Deboragh, he pulls Jennifer into the bathroom and starts kissing and groping her.

"You're getting married, right?" Jenny asked, confused but not resisting and in fact already in love with me.

"Supposed to be," I replied, lifting her dress.

"So how come you're kissing me like this?"

It was a good question. I wanted to possess Deboragh, but I wanted to *know* Jennifer. She knew famous actors and musicians. She'd seen things. She'd been there, you know? And I envied that.

"I guess I want it all," I finally answered.

Before we got any further, Deboragh came home. Right away she smelled trouble. Sniffed the funny business before she got upstairs. She wanted me to fire Jenny, but I played it smooth, saying that was fine with me, but then she'd have to take over the redecorating. Knowing Deboragh was a grandiose bitch who never did a day's work in her life, I prayed that she would react in character—which she did.

"Well, maybe we should keep her around just to finish up," she said.

"Uh, good idea," I replied. "Okay."

The wedding, if you can call such a spectacle that, took place the next day—barely. I was drunk. My daughter Elizabeth wore black. Pam Grier showed up uninvited. And Deboragh, the bride, who was an hour late and had to be revived after taking too many Quaaludes, said, "Thank God you were drunk when I got there, because if you'd seen what I looked like..."

The following morning I showed up on the set of "The Richard Pryor Show" still wearing my wedding tux, ready to tape the third of four shows.

By then, I was already resigned to failure. Not only were we pitted against "Happy Days" and "Laverne and Shirley," the two top-rated shows, but the network censors thwarted me from the git-go. On the very first show, they refused to air the opening bit, a close-up of me reporting how delighted I was to have my own show.

"There's been a lot of things written about me," I said with a straight face. "People ask, 'How can you have a show? You'll have to compromise."

At that point, the camera panned back and showed me standing naked (I was in a body stocking), with my balls cut off.

"Well, look at me," I continued. "I've given up absolutely nothing."

With a supporting cast that included Robin Williams, Sandra Bernhard, and Marsha Warfield, we still managed to deliver an exciting, surprising, and provocative show. In one skit, I played the first black president of the United States, who's asked at a press conference if he planned on continuing to see white women. After revealing the strain of such a delicate subject, he replied, "As long as I can keep it up."

Then he added, "Why do you think it's called the White House?"

The show was no vanilla milkshake. It was poignant: In one sketch, a wino returned home to his wife, who was played by writer Maya Angelou. She used her Pulitzer Prize-winning genius to elevate this takeoff on my "Nigger with a Seizure" routine into a monologue about the woeful self-destruction by black males.

The show also had its share of punch lines: As a slick black evangelist with a global-sized Afro, I groused about not having the "crossover buck, the Billy Graham dollars."

I'm proud of the effort. But the medium's limitations were as frustrating as low ratings. The show also took a tremendous toll on my health. My drugging, drinking, and relationship excesses were lethal when combined with the pressure of being a perfectionist and putting on a weekly series.

I imagined resting when Debbie and I finally honeymooned in Maui, but it was nothing to put on a postcard home. I spent the first night drunk and covered with vomit in a shower while she complained about the awful condition of the bungalow we had reserved. It was old, there were bugs, and the hotel didn't provide room service.

"Are we going to eat cornflakes for a week?" Debbie asked.

I attempted to redeem myself the next evening by going to the grocery store and cooking fried chicken, mashed potatoes, and corn on the cob. But it was a temporary reprieve.

At the end of October the craziness began all over again when I went to work on *The Wiz* in New York. I couldn't help myself. I caroused with sleazy, doped-up nogoodniks all night. I was as lit as the white suit I wore playing the Wiz himself. I answered my wake-up calls by saying, "Oh, shit, I made it again."

I didn't realize the extent to which I was wreaking havoc on my system and jeopardizing my health until I went to Peoria in early November for my grandmother's seventy-eighth birthday. The fall weather was brisk and energizing. But I was wiped out. Too many drugs, too little sleep, too much work, too many problems.

Still, I fell immediately back into my old habits, much to Deboragh's chagrin. One afternoon she and I, Uncle Dickie, and my grandmother went fishing, and in the middle of the outing Uncle Dickie and I disappeared with what Debbie described as the "two most unattractive white women ever—dogs."

She was packing to go back to L.A. when the phone rang. "Deboragh," Uncle Dickie said, "Richard's had a heart attack."

To be sure, I'd almost gone the way of my dad. Bit the bullet with an ugly whore. My heart had begun palpitating. I'd gotten sick and had trouble breathing. But even then I didn't give it much attention.

"Hi, Rich."

Then the pain arrived.

It was late getting to the party.

If the other shit didn't get my attention, that did.

"Oh, fuck!"

Never mind that I'd been on the cover of *Newsweek* or hailed by *Time* as the new black superstar. Never mind my latest picture, *Which Way Is Up?* opened that week. Never mind I had money, a mansion, women, and cars.

I got my ass home and hollered like a kid: "Mama! Mama! Help me, Mama!"

Them motherfuckers hurt. I don't care what nobody tells your ass. I was walking in the yard and someone say, "Don't breathe no more."

I said, "Huh?"

He said, "Don't breathe no motherfucking more. You heard me."

"Okay, I won't breathe. I won't breathe."

I tried to ease a little air inside my mouth. Then I heard, "Say, motherfucker, didn't I tell you not to breathe?"

"You told me not to breathe."

"Well, why you walking? Stand still, motherfucker."

"Okay."

"Get your ass down."

"Okay, I'm down. I'm down. Don't hurt me."

"Shut the fuck up. You thinkin' 'bout dyin', huh?"

"Yeah, yeah. Dyin'."

"Why didn't you think about that when you was eatin' that pork, motherfucker? Drinking that whiskey and snortin' that cocaine, motherfucker?"

My family worried themselves sick. They were probably closer to death than I was. They saw their money supply gasping for air, moaning and writhing in pain. They probably wondered if this wasn't some sick joke. Me coming home to die in front of them. They weren't going to have none of that shit. Not about to lose my fame and money.

They called an ambulance. Told them to get into the ghetto quick. Told them a white woman had been shot.

I woke up in the ambulance and I was looking at nothing but white people staring down at me. I said, "Oh, God, I fucked around and wound up in the wrong motherfucking heaven. Now I got to listen to Lawrence Welk the rest of my days."

I spent four days at the hospital in ICU, where doctors determined I'd had a "scare" rather than an attack. My grandmother gave all sorts of explanations to the press, ranging from too much smothered steak and cabbage to a heart scare. No one mentioned a family history of heart disease or the chance that my ticker didn't enjoy the "white lady"—cocaine—as much as I did.

No one mentioned anything.

The doctors simply told me to take it easy.

"Remember, Mr. Pryor, moderation."

"Right. No problem."

23

OUR NEW YEAR'S PARTY STARTED OUT LIKE EVERYONE ELSE'S. Debbie and I invited a bunch of friends over to celebrate as the clock ticked past midnight. We drank and snorted cocaine and kissed as the calendar changed to 1978. But none of us anticipated starting the new year with a blast.

By morning, though, I was plastered. Debbie and I were also fighting like cats and dogs. Then she threatened to take off with her girlfriends, all of whom sat on one side of the living room snickering at me. Being someone who didn't take kindly to insults on my manhood, I went for the ultimate fuck-you:

My .357 Magnum.

I grabbed it from my nightstand table. Then I waved it in her face. Didn't bother Debbie one bit. She refused to flinch. Stayed right in front of me. I said to myself, "This bitch is crazy, you know?"

"You gonna shoot something, shoot me," Debbie said.

I took most challenges, but not this one. I pointed the gun away from her. She moved in front of it.

"Deboragh, stop!" I said

"Then put the gun down now," she demanded.

"Fuck you."

I ordered Deboragh and her friends outside. Not that anything changed. We just yelled at each other in the driveway. A moment later, they decided enough was enough and made a beeline for my Mercedes, obviously planning a speedy getaway. But I stopped that by jumping between them and opening fire on my car.

I thought it was fair myself. My wife was going to leave me. I said, "Not in this motherfucker, you ain't. You may be leaving, but you gonna be walking away from this motherfucker because I'm gonna kill this here. So go get them Hush Puppies and get your ass down the road.

Then I opened fire.

I shot one of them tires. Boom! That tire said, "Ahhhhh." Sounded good to me. I shot another one. "Ohhhhhhh."
The vodka I was drinking said, "Go ahead, shoot something else."
I shot the motor. But the motor fell out. The motor said, "Fuck it."

I was the last one who could explain why I did such a stupid thing, but apparently "I'm sorry" wasn't enough. One of the womens called the police. If you want to get a cop to respond quickly, all you have to say is, 'Hello, Officer, I want to report a black man with a gun." It's like announcing the start of hunting season at an NRA convention. The cops arrived so fast I barely had time to run inside and smoke all my dope.

Then the police came. I went into the house. 'Cuz they got Magnums, too. And they don't kill cars.
They kill nig-gars.

They arrested me for assault with a deadly weapon. I went to jail and was freed on bail later that day. The charges were dropped in February.

Within six months, Deboragh and I were officially divorced and back to being friends. I probably should've given my love life a vacation. Maybe taken a decade or two off. Instead I grabbed hold of Jenny and lulled her into the calm center of my hurricane.

"What's wrong?" she said. "Are you trying to catch a train?"

It was the first time we made love.

"What do you mean?" I asked.

"Slow down," she said. "Slow down."

I wish it had been possible.

From the beginning Jennifer and I were mismatched lovers who couldn't get over thinking how lucky we were to have found each other. She came into the picture knowing exactly what to say and do to inspire my mind and excite the rest of me. To her, I was one in a million, a prince who didn't see his royal standing.

And I felt elevated around Jenny. In this well-bred, college-educated beauty, I thought I might've found somebody who could love me so hard and passionately that I'd finally be able to love myself. But our relationship was marred by a tragic weakness that would nearly destroy both of us.

Jenny was almost as big a dope dummy as me. In a test of wills, she was as strong and stubborn as me. She drank with me. She snorted coke with me. But the worst of our secrets was shared the first time I slapped her.

When a man hits a woman one of two things happens: either she hauls ass in the opposite direction or she becomes yours.

Violence is like voodoo. The sting is like a hex. You become possessed by each other. Locked in a diabolic dance.

I lived in that dark place you go when you grow up with people telling you that you aren't worth shit, and Jennifer, bless her heart, followed me down that destructive path. Whether we were vacationing in Maui, locked behind the gates at my house, or on the road, we never left that faraway place where passion met brutality.

It gripped us both equally. I broke furniture. She threw bottles. We ripped each other's clothes. Even the lighter, innocent moments were tinged with red. One night we were in my study when I leaned across the desk and told her that I wanted to suck her pussy.

"Say that again and I'll hit you in the nose," she said.

I scooted closer.

I spoke slower.

"I—want—to—suck—your—pussy."

Suddenly she popped me in the face.

Boom!

I smothered the sting with my hand and saw that it was covered with blood. Jenny ran downstairs and roused all 350 pounds of my Uncle Dickie from in front of the TV in the kitchen.

"Help me! Help me!" she screamed. "I hit Richard and he's bleeding!"

Uncle Dickie hadn't budged when I entered the scene.

"Where is she? I'm gonna kill the bitch!"

Moments later it was like nothing happened. I apologized. I promised it wouldn't happen again.

"Just stay with me, baby," I said. "Don't leave."

And she didn't.

I didn't excuse such behavior. In all honesty, I didn't even think about it. From as far back as I can remember, I saw men handle their women with a certain roughness. One time, as a child, I followed my father and stepmother up the stairs of our house, watching as my dad beat the crap out of Viola. It was very upsetting. It wasn't a fair fight. I knew he shouldn't have been beating her.

"Daddy, don't hit her," I pleaded. "Don't hit her no more."

He turned around.

"This is my woman," he snapped. "Now you get your ass back down those steps and mind your own business."

I remember my mother and father was fighting once and I was going to jump in, Jack. Not my mother, motherfucker!

But he beat the shit out of me.

"Nigger, what the fuck?"

"That's my mama!"

"That's my woman, motherfucker!"

I never understood. I always wondered if maybe she liked him kicking her ass. Or maybe it was a man thing to do.

It wasn't until later I realized that letting them go is the man thing to do.

But it's hard to be that strong.

When I took Jenny to Peoria, it was to show her all the sights and people of my youth, the places where I'd grown up and hung out. I wanted her to see what I couldn't describe, the smells and details, the colors and the sounds. But whether or not I realized it, I was also putting her in the midst of my long-time struggle to break free from the past that was often more powerful than I was able to admit.

From their visits to L.A., I already knew most of my family weren't too fond of Jenny. They sensed she had the grit and determination to help me pull away from them, and they feared that more than anything. Mine was a family of survivors. They enjoyed my fame and fortune. They were extremely happy that I'd made a better life for myself. But at the same time they felt that my success also entitled them to a better life.

So when Jenny and I settled into Mama's, they made sure that I knew my place. Mama served soul food. Uncle Dickie started a poker game. Cousins, aunts and uncles, and friends of theirs appeared from out of nowhere. The hours passed. Jenny went to bed. Dickie arranged for womens to come by. The sun rose and they started the same shit all over again.

"Never forget where you came from, Rich."

"'Member your roots, son."

"Where would ya be if not for all the material we've been givin' you? Shit, I feel like I wrote half your act."

I could only take so much. Then I burst.

I looked at Mama. At the others. I was famous. The *New York Times* loved me. I lived in a mansion with a swimming pool and tennis court. I'd bought some of these people their homes, paid their mortgages, given them cars.

None of it mattered.

Suddenly I was crying like a baby.

"You never loved me. Ever since I was a little boy you wanted me to be a pimp. I couldn't do it."

At thirty-eight years old, I was crying the tears they never let me. The tears I never let myself cry.

"Let me be who I am, goddamn it. You want me to be like all of you, stuck here in Peoria, doing nothing with your lives."

Mama tried calming me down.

"And you took me away from my mother," I continued. "I loved her. Didn't you know that, Mama?"

A few hours later Mama got me one of her whores and I left Jenny alone with her guitar, to sing the blues.

Our blues.

That was the drill. The tug of war. I apologized and we went back home to L.A. Then something happened inside me. One summer night Jennifer and I were driving home from a dinner party at a friend's house when I abruptly turned the car around and drove to the Comedy Store. I hadn't been there for months, but when we arrived there I waited my turn and then climbed on stage and ended a long drought between standup performances.

Bonded by a great sense of purpose—me delivering the best comedy of my career—Jenny and I became inseparable. Even dependent on each other. Jenny picked out my clothes. She dressed me in Armani suits and made sure to stick a gardenia in my jacket lapel before I went on stage. She sat in the back of the Comedy Store and took notes. In the morning we ate breakfast by the pool and critiqued and honed routines that became the heart of my concert movie: *Wanted: Richard Pryor Live in Concert* to comedy perfection.

Jenny praised me for telling the truth, for being able to take my life and turn it into a funny theater of the absurd. However, it wasn't only me. My life worked for me. For instance, before Jenny and I went on vacation in Hana, she fired the housekeeper and replaced her with the weekend maid. A few days later the maid telephoned us in Hawaii, sobbing and hysterical. She'd left my cousin's Great Dane in the backyard with my miniature horse, Ginger.

"Oh, Mr. Pryor," she cried. "Ginger was eaten. The dogs ate her."

I remember the first time the dogs saw the horse. They thought it was another dog. My cousin had a Great Dane staying with us. They ran over to see the horse and then that smell hit their ass.

"Hey, that ain't no goddamn dog."

"You smell that shit? Ain't no dog in the world shit like that, Jack."

Great Dane say, "I don't know what it is, but I'm gonna fuck it."

Come back and say, "Can't fuck it."

Other one say, "Well, let's eat the bitch."

One night Jenny and I made love. First, I had an orgasm and she didn't. I pounded my chest. She called me Macho Man.

I don't give a damn if you come or not, 'cause I'm Macho Man.

Then she had an orgasm.

And you can tell when you made good love to your woman, right? 'Cause she will go to sleep.

That's when you really are Macho Man.

One day Jenny demanded credit for that bit.

I said, "Go register it at the Writers Guild. Then we'll talk."

After working all summer at the Comedy Store, I set out on a large tour that fall. The halls sold out. The reviews were worshipful. There was nothing better than spending an hour and a half on stage, making people laugh. With the comedy gods smiling down on me, I was in heaven.

But the feeling was short-lived. The time I spent by myself between shows was hellish. I hated being alone. I was my own worst company. After one show, David Banks and I were hustled by bodyguards to a waiting limo. A moment later, I ordered the driver to turn around and the bodyguards to relax.

"You did too good of a job," I said to them. "Now we're gonna go back and this time let a few womens through, okay?"

Fortunately, Jenny was with me most of the time. She encouraged me to read books, visit museums, and see shows. She kept me fully engaged in real life rather than allowing me to indulge my inclination to sit in a darkened room, doing dope and entertaining lowlifes.

Sometimes her task was easy. Other times we fought without remorse.

The year closed on a dark note. At the end of December, my grandmother suffered a severe stroke. Gravely ill, she didn't appear long for the world. Jenny and I flew to Peoria so I could be by her bedside.

Even then I was conflicted between past and present, between my family and my future. Knowing my grandmother didn't like Jennifer, I nonetheless escorted her into the hospital room to sit with me. Seeing my grandmother dying was difficult for me to face. I needed Jenny's support, and I said so.

"Mama," I said, motioning toward Jenny, "this is the woman I love."

Rather than respond, she reached out and touched my overcoat, which she had bought me. She rubbed it with two brittle, bent fingers.

"Are you cold, Mama?" I asked.

Her lips moved, but I couldn't hear what she was saying. Then Jenny filled me in on what was really going on.

"She's not cold, Richard," she whispered. "She just wants to be loving. She's trying to love you."

That was nice, Mama.

"It feels like blue azure," Mama managed to say.

"Yes, Mama. And it's warm. Very warm. Thank you."

Though sick and inches from death, she was still a formidable woman in her own way. Her doctors were trying to put a tube up inside her, but she wasn't letting them. Desperate to help, I stood in the doorway, tears running down my face, and told her that if she didn't let them work on her, I'd do it myself.

Before I left, I saw her relax.

I guess she knew.

I never saw anyone deal with death like that. I mean, serene and shit, you know? Me, I'd be screaming, "Death, get the fuck away from me!" But Marie, she took it calmly. A few hours after I left her room, she died.

Yes, she did. She died.

And that was something.

24

FIVE YEARS EARLIER I HAD LOOKED OUT FROM THE COVER OF A record album with a funny face and a wry look in my eyes and said, "That nigger's crazy." It had been a joke. But after Mama died, nothing struck me as funny.

The world was mine. My concert movie *Wanted* was an instant smash after opening in October. Reviewers seemed grateful that, after so many big-screen misfires, my brand of humor had finally been successfully captured on film. Then Hollywood, which loves a hit movie, also seemed to rediscover me.

Surely I wasn't white.

Suddenly I wasn't black either.

I was green.

But as Kermit the Frog said, "It's not easy being green."

Projects were heaped at my feet. A sequel to *The Sting* with Lily Tomlin. Neil Simon wanted to write *Macho Man* for his wife Marsha Mason and me. Producer Ray Stark brought me *The Toy* and *Family Dreams*. Through my own deals with studios, I talked about developing a movie based on George Orwell's *Animal Farm* and remaking *Arsenic and Old Lace*. I was also offered the lead in a film based on the life of jazz great Charlie Parker.

But it seemed too much to handle. Instead of taking advantage of being a hot commodity, I was awash in a depression that crashed over me following Mama's death. I truly felt as if I was flailing underwater, stuck in a surreal nightmare.

Despite whatever problems I had dealing with my grandmother, she had always been my anchor, my tether to some sense of reality, and with her gone I began drifting and floating over the landscape without any court.

It was like the word game I'd played with Chevy Chase on *Saturday Night Live.*

"Mama."

"Dead."

"Life."

"Death."

"Richard."

No one dared think about how I might respond to that suggestion, except for Jennifer. The flow of hookers and my frequent all-night, sometimes week-long disappearances into the squalid home of a strung-out female drug dealer who plied me with my life's two essentials told her I was in trouble. These flights occurred every night rather than every now and then. Yet she stayed at my side. Put up with me. Berated me. And dragged my ass home.

Any doubt that I was on a path to self-destruction was erased the day I emerged from the bath with half my mustache shaved off, then dressed in a red jogging suit, silver shoes, and a top hat, and announced that I was going out.

"Oh, really," she said. "Where ya goin'?"

"Shuffling off to Buffalo," I grinned madly.

After that, she checked my ass into a hospital. It was clear the egg had cracked.

In the hospital, I spent a few days detoxing while under the thumb of some good sedatives — a contradiction in terms if you want my opinion, though I wasn't complaining. Once my eyes cleared, I began talking to a psychiatrist, a scholarly-looking black man who made me realize how affected I was by my grandmother's death. I'd told myself it didn't bother me, but it did.

"Everybody's dying around me," I said. "It makes me scared."

Ironically, I had a hard time in the therapist's office. All I had to do was talk about myself, but I found that painfully difficult. I figured it was too personal. But God bless him, the man tried.

"What exactly about cocaine do you like?" he asked.

"It fucks me up good. I like that ping it puts in my head."

"Do you see how it removes you from reality? Mentally as well as physically? You spend days and even weeks isolated in your house, alone in your bedroom, getting high."

"Yeah, but that's okay."

"Why's that? Why's it okay?"

"I don't see any need to be in reality because I've seen how ugly the world is."

He didn't buy that shit. Not for an instant. Wanted to know how I was so confident of the world's ugliness when I wouldn't venture into it and check things out. He started asking me where I'd been, the places I thought were ugly, places I thought were nice, and finally, as if setting me up, he asked how I could make such extreme statements about the world when I'd never been to the origin of the world's beauty.

Okay, I bit.

"Where's that?" I asked.

"Africa."

Excited after reading Richard Leakey's and Roger Lewin's *Origins*, Jennifer and I left for Kenya on Easter Sunday, 1979. From the moment we touched down at the small airport in Mombasa, I sensed something extraordinary. Through the jet lag, I knew something was different but couldn't articulate it. Couldn't get good reception. I strained to hear a beat that was too far away. However, I realized the shrink had been right. The place really was beautiful.

My eyes were full.

It was so beautiful. It was black. Blue black. Original black. The kind of place where you go, "Black."

And landing at the airport in Nairobi, it just fills your heart up. You see everybody's black. And you realize that people are the same all over the world. Because people in Africa fuck over your luggage just like people in New York.

The next day we went to Nairobi, where the sensation of being in Africa grew even stronger. Something was indeed different, exciting, alive, but radically so. We took a tour of the National Museum, and that completely rearranged the cells in my brain. Did a whole rewiring trip on me. By the time I sat my ass down in the hotel lobby, I knew what I was feeling.

"Jennifer," I said. "You know what? There are no niggers here."

She glanced around the hotel lobby. It was full of gorgeous black people, like everyplace else we'd been. The only people you saw were black. At the hotel, on television, in stores, on the street, in the newspapers, at restaurants, running the government, on advertisements. Everywhere.

"There are no niggers here," I repeated. "The people here, they still have their self-respect, their pride."

Over the next week, we traveled into the bush. Settled into a lodge in the middle of Masai territory. I loved their attractiveness, their ancient yet timeless tribal look, their ornate beads, their twisted, elongated earlobes, their pride and grandeur, and the way they stood guard over an earth that belonged to them before it belonged to any other humans.

The animals were a different story. We went on a safari. Not to shoot, only to look. But we still went deep into the jungle, driving until it felt as if we had driven to a different planet. It was so pretty, and there were no people. Just monkeys, giraffes, elephants, hippos, jackals, and lions. Moving in packs, kicking up dust, looking for food.

I couldn't take my eyes off a lion that was tearing into a Cape buffalo. Motherfucker ate like my dad.

"Oh, goddamn, this is good. Shit. Goddamn."

It was no zoo.

We all go to the zoo and fuck with the lions, cause the lion can't get out. You say, "Hey, lion! Hey, motherfucker!"

But when you see a pride of lions, about twenty of them motherfuckers, hanging out, they have a different attitude. They see you and say, "Yeah, get your ass out of the car. Bring the camera, too. 'Cause we gonna eat all of that shit."

After three weeks, I had no doubt that being in Africa had had a profound effect on me. It seemed especially so when it came time to return to the United States. The land had been timeless, the people majestic. I had seen and felt things impossible to experience any place else on Earth. I left enlightened.

I also left regretting ever having uttered the word "nigger" on a stage or off it. It was a wretched word. Its connotations weren't funny, even when people laughed. To this day I wish I'd never said the word. I felt its lameness. It was misunderstood by people. They didn't get what I was talking about.

Neither did I.

I wished that I'd kept my mouth shut.

But that was a hard thing to do. An impossible thing to do.

It wasn't too late, though.

And so I vowed never to say it again.

One thing that happened to me that was magic was that I was leaving, sitting in the hotel lobby, and a voice said, "What do you see? Look around." And I looked around, and I looked around, and I saw people of all colors and shapes and the voice said, "You see any niggers?"

I said, "No."

It said, "You know why? 'Cause there aren't any."

'Cause I'd been there three weeks and hadn't said it. And it started making me cry, man. All that shit. All the acts I've been doing. As an artist and comedian. Speaking and trying to say something. And I been saying that. That's a devastating fucking word. That has nothing to do with us. We are from a place where they first started people.

In Africa.

In Kenya.

Dr. Leakey, a white anthropologist — which I have to say so white people will believe me — he found remains of a man that stood up and walked on earth 5 million years ago. You know that motherfucker didn't speak French.

I mean, black people — we are the first motherfuckers on the planet.

My epiphany was highly personal. I would do what I could to make my feelings known at home. It was a vision that extended beyond black people and included people of all colors. My comedy was color-blind. None of it would've ever worked if the world was all one color.

I mean, even black ain't beautiful if it's the only color you look at every day. Life's richness, its beauty and excitement, come from the diversity of things. The multitude of colors that greet you when you step outside the door each day.

I no longer wanted to be someone who pointed out the dif-ferences—especially racial ones.

I wanted to help people see how similar all of us are.

I came back home and thought of Malcolm's turnaround at the end and how beautiful it was and how people considered him a traitor for it, and it made me teary-eyed all over again because he had been right.

We're all just people.

We're all the same.

What else I found out in Africa is the fact that aside from us being the original people, so are the white people.

We all family.

That's it, Jack. And fuck all that other shit. 'Cause it don't mean nothing except about some cash.

25

HOLY SHIT.

I didn't expect the reaction I got when I disavowed the word "nigger." Mooney and David Banks told me that people thought I'd gone soft, sold out, turned my back on the cause, and all that political, militant shit. I received death threats. Kooks showed up at my house, threw shit over the gate. I got letters. And comments from people who thought they owned me and didn't want me to stray.

It was the same struggle I had with my family when they said, "Don't forget where you came from."

They wanted my voice to be theirs.

And they didn't want mine to change.

But I wasn't Malcolm, Martin, or anybody else. I was a drug-addicted, paranoid, frightened, lonely, sad, and frustrated comedian who had gotten too big for his britches. I'd wanted laughs, not racial struggles. I'd wanted to be liked, not hated. Overburdened, I'd walked too far out onto the wing, lifted too much weight, and finally I buckled under the pressure.

I was terrified of the jacket.

Confused, I squandered away the summer, working two days for $50,000 on the lame comedy *In God We Trust* and preparing for a major role co-starring with Cicely Tyson in *Family Dreams* (later retitled *Bustin' Loose*). But neither picture, when it came to facing facts, was of the caliber I should've been doing if my head hadn't been lost in a haze of vodka, coke, and anger.

As it was, my finest performances were at home. Jenny and I acted like schizophrenic lovebirds: passionate one moment, attempting to murder each other the next. Calling the cops, then persuading them nothing was wrong. This woman turned out to be just as tough and crazed as me. My Uncle Dickie used to say, "You know why? 'Cuz the Irish are niggers turned inside out."

Seemingly destined for the Domestic Violence Hall of Fame, we nearly rewrote the record book the night I stood in the living room, cranked to the gills, and grabbed my .357 revolver. I fired three rounds, then turned and pointed the gun at Jenny, and ordered, "Get out, bitch." Thirty minutes later, when we made up, I said, "I'm glad you didn't make me kill you."

It was classic.

I was the victim.

Nothing was my fault.

I offered no apologies. Take my behavior on the set of *Family Dreams* in Seattle that October. Erratic and ornery from dope, I must've worn out Cicely to the point where she spoke to her husband, who called me one afternoon in my trailer and in his own way asked me to shape up.

"Rich," he said.

Only one man in the world had that voice.

"Miles!"

"Rich. That's my woman."

Then he hung up.

Even so, I knew what he meant. But I was too far into the shit. Sorry, brother.

Needless to say, going to Dirty Dick's meant I had one thing on my mind, and it was no secret to anybody, because I was so goddamn open about using cocaine that it had become a cornerstone of my act, such as it was. When I walked into his place one afternoon in November, 1978, I saw him going through this complicated process to fix up a tiny rock of 100 percent pure coke and then smoke it.

It transfixed me. My feet might as well have been in cement blocks. I stared and tried to comprehend the nuances of the ritual. It was like watching someone do a new dance step. It looked cool, the expression on his face, total bliss, real out there, and when the motherfucker came down from that rocket blast, he looked at me like he'd just come.

"Oh, man," he said.

"Yeah?"

"Yeah, Rich. You know, I just seen God."

"God?"

"Motherfucking God."

When I first did it, I knew it was going to fuck me up, but I had to do it. Had to be hip. Motherfucker said, "You ever try this?"

I thought, He's going to string me out. He's a dope dealer who needs me to get hooked so he can get some freebase. This dude used to snort a little coke. But I saw him and said, "What's wrong with you?"

He said, "Have you ever freebased?"

"Say what?"

"Freebased?"

He told me he saw Jesus.

Dirty Dick didn't have to ask if I wanted to try it. From the look in my eye, he just started to cook the rock.

"I'll do everything," he said. "You just suck on the pipe. Like it was a chick's dick."

Honest to God, I was scared that first time. I thought it was going to be something else. But it was nice.

That was the worst part.

That it was nice.

◆   ◆   ◆

In a terribly ominous, ironic forewarning of the calamity that lay ahead, I started a fire that first time I freebased at home. The rambling house was still, dark, and quiet. I was by myself, behind closed doors in my bedroom, seated at a little table, chasing that first high. Rock, lighter, rum, pipe. I thought that I was in touch with the Lord.

"Oh, Jesus," I muttered. "Oh, God."

I should've sensed right then the magic pipe was more than I could handle. But you don't have any sense when you smoke that shit.

Jenny told me that when she came home the place had the feel of a haunted house. If it wasn't ugly before, it was then. Strange. Spooky. Menace in the air. I heard her call me, but I didn't respond. When she walked into the bedroom, I was standing beside the bed, pipe in hand, and staring at the pink comforter, which was on fire. The room was filled with smoke. Flames danced at my feet as if grasping for me.

"Richard!" she screamed.

My assistant, Rashon, ran in, grabbed the burning blanket, and took it outside. From numbsville, I tried to explain.

"I don't know what happened. I was just trying to light the pipe the way you're supposed to. But the rum on the cotton tip must've dropped on the blanket and…"

As I dove deeper into the gloom, I corrupted those around me, missed a $100,000, one-day cameo in the biblical spoof *Wholly Moses*, and barely noticed Christmas and New Year's. In less than a year, I'd gone from my artistic peak to personal pits.

I didn't give a fuck.

Didn't even notice.

It started out innocently enough. Every now and then. A little bit. "Naw, not now. No base. Fuck it." Pretty soon, I noticed I wasn't walking as far away from the pipe as I used to. I used to put the pipe down and go, "I'll be in here." Then motherfuckers you used to share with come by and you say, "Hey, ain't you got some of your own shit?"

If you're unlucky, you sit and wait for someone to fix your rocks, and that's all you think about—when am I going to get my turn? The person who cooks has got all the power. I was fortunate. I had money. I cooked it myself. I was fascinated with shaking up the shit, cooking it, watching it bubble down, you know?

I was like a kid watching magic.

Performing it myself.

Spellbound by the power of turning powder to rock.

You put it on the paper end and—*dink*—it would be a rock, you know.

I was out one night and we was doing it and a woman says, 'The fire don't last long enough." We kept trying to get it, and I said, "What kind of fire do you want?"

The dude says, "The kind that lasts forever."

You want to know the difference between sniffing and smoking?

Snorting you get high.

With base, you hope you don't die.

Bill Cosby had once said of me that the line between comedy and tragedy was a thin one. From where I stood on the eve of filming *Stir Crazy* in Tucson in early March, there was no line. My mind was somewhere other than on this crazy caper about two truck drivers who bust out of prison after being mistakenly convicted of robbery.

I immediately set myself apart from co-star, Gene Wilder, and director, Sidney Poitier. Rather than stay in the luxury hotel where they were encamped, I rented a ramshackle home in the hills that was as isolated as I was trying to make myself. My unwillingness to play team ball created tension as thick as the smoke in the pipe that prevented me from showing up for work until noon or later. Another fuck-up.

If unprofessionalism had been my only indiscretion, I might not have made so many enemies. But I lived up to my badass reputation by trying to make friends with the prisoners at the Arizona State Penitentiary, showing them that I was cool by getting them water and even sneaking them drugs.

Shit, Richard, what were you trying to prove?

I always said the black man had been fucked over in the revolution. We're nice people. We just got a bad break. But I was there six weeks and I talked to some of the brothers there. Thank God we got penitentiaries.

I said to one, "Why'd you kill everybody in the house?"

He said, "They was home."

Although I was lucky to make it through the movie, I was even luckier not to have landed in jail alongside the murderers, thieves, and drug addicts like myself when I started buying coke through a connection with some motorcycle gangbangers. Unbeknownst to me, they were being monitored by state police and federal agents, including their visits to and from my trailer and my hillside home.

We became targets, too. One night Jennifer smelled cigarette smoke. Then we heard the crunch of gravel outside my house. It wasn't merely my paranoia. Jennifer had been sober for months. We definitely were being watched. The next day, agents and cops were all over the set. For the first time that I knew of, I was in danger of getting busted.

My dumb-ass solution?

Confrontation.

Show them who was hip.

"I hear you guys are mad at me," I said to one of the federal narcs. "Sorry."

They didn't give a shit about my sorry ass.

"We suggest you don't buy any more dope while you're here," he said. "And if you try to leave the state with any, we'll arrest you."

Fair warning. But I couldn't help but do whatever stash was left before returning to L.A. I even got to the airport, then ordered the driver to turn around so I could go back and dig up the emergency stuff I'd buried in the yard.

Nobody can talk you out of doing shit when you've made up your mind to hurt yourself, right?

As the movie finished in L.A., Jenny left me. To her, it was a life-and-death decision. She feared the base was going to kill her if she didn't escape.

My bitch left me and I went crazy.

I was convinced that Jennifer was cheating on me. That's why she left. That's what was really driving me crazy. At first, I hired various dealer lackeys to tail her. Then one night I decided to punish her myself. I trapped her in the bedroom and nearly strangled her to death while repeating, "Jenny Lee, today you're going to die."

But I fell in love with this pipe. The pipe controlled my very being. This motherfucker say, "Don't answer the phone. We have smoking to do." Or the pipe's talking about "Now come on, don't put me down anyplace where I might fall. Because it's two in the morning and it's hard to get one of me."

I had the same suspicions about people who worked for me. I feared they were stealing money from me, making business deals I didn't understand. I didn't know whether I was paranoid or not. In my state of mind it didn't matter. But just to be safe, I began withdrawing large sums of money from the bank and hiding it in lock boxes at home.

I was high around-the-clock.

I was paranoid.

I was sad.

I cooked up base in the kitchen and ran to my bedroom where I smoked it.

I had conversations in my mind with everybody. Entertainers. Presidents. All of them.

That was a strange place.

I was doing so much I embarrassed cocaine dealers. They said, "Richard, man, goddamn. Come on. Shit. Why don't you just snort the shit?" "Okay, yeah, I'll just snort it." "How much you want?" "A kilo. Just for the weekend."

Football Hall of Famer Jim Brown tried to intervene.

Jim Brown asked, "What are you doing?"
"Freebase."
"What's free about it?"

After cooking up a fresh batch of rocks one night, I walked from the kitchen toward the bedroom. To get there, though, I needed to walk down a long hallway. About halfway through, I was confronted by an apparition. At first, it was too far in front, dancing through the walls too quickly for me to get a long, clear look.

As I took another step, it sprang out from the wall right in front of me and I saw that it was me. Skinny, orange-skinned, wearing black underwear. I was the devil. I pranced around myself in fiery circles, playing, laughing, closing in, weirded-out.

Eight months before, when Dirty Dick had started me freebasing, he promised I'd see God.

Motherfucker. Look who showed up instead.

The devil.

"Are you really me?" I asked.

"Yes, I am you," the devil incarnate said.

Then he—rather, I—disappeared inside the wall again. In the instant, I sprinted into the bedroom and locked the door. I fought the urge to open it a crack and look back, certain that if I did, I would die.

The motherfucker.

And I knew why he was there, too.

He wanted to kill me. Put my ass out of its misery.

26

AFTER FREEBASING WITHOUT INTERRUPTION FOR SEVERAL DAYS in a row, I wasn't able to discern one for the next. Night and day became different shades of gray. Nor did I care about such details as time. But after waking from a short, unrefreshing, troubled sleep late on the morning of June 9, I drove into Hollywood, where I entered my bank and demanded all the cash from several large accounts I had there.

My brain was strung out. That morning's smoke-a-thon rekindled my paranoia that people were stealing from me.

I wanted my money.

While I was ineffectually arguing with the bank manager, who explained that they needed prior notice for such a transaction, Jennifer called my house and pleaded with my Aunt Dee to get me help. She'd never seen me so wasted and sickly. When Aunt Dee reassured her that I was fine, Jenny made a beeline out to Northridge in order to confront me herself. But the sight of me in the dark, clutching my pipe, told her it was useless.

"I know what I have to do," I mumbled. "I've brought shame to my family. I've hurt you. I've destroyed my career. I know what I have to do."

Shortly after she frustrated herself out the door, Deboragh phoned me. We hadn't spoken for almost a year, but she felt compelled to check and see how I was doing. It was as if she and Jenny, the two people who didn't give a damn about my power trips or being cut off, sensed it was time to say goodbye. They knew it was a scary time.

"You're the only one I trust," I told her. "They're trying to get my money."

"Who is?" she asked.

"It's not fun anymore," I mumbled.

"What's not fun, Richard?"

"I don't think I can get out of here, you know?"

The house was full. From Rashon to my cousin and Aunt Dee, not to mention the housekeepers and cook, people were doing their thing. They were trained to leave me alone. Oh, Mr. Pryor, he's in his bedroom. They didn't mention that the door was locked. By late afternoon, the only reason to suspect I was present was the continuous smell of acrid smoke and the foreboding vibes that sent into the rest of the house.

Nothing changed as darkness took the heat out of the beautiful spring day. Hovered over my rocks, pipe, cognac, and Bic lighter, I smoked and soared and crashed and smoked again, repeating the deadly cycle over and over again as if I was chain-smoking Marlboros. But I didn't allow time even for cigarettes. I'd never felt more paranoid, depressed, or hopeless.

Hopeless.

As if I was drowning.

Voices swirled in my head so that I wasn't able to tell which came from me and which were hallucinations. My conversations became animated, like those crazy people on the street. I heard people who had worked for me talking outside the bedroom window. They were loud, rude, laughing, angry. They made fun of my helplessness. I yelled at them, louder and louder, and still they refused to answer.

"What the fuck are you doing out there?"

As that craziness went on, I continued to smoke until I ran out of cocaine. By then, I was experiencing serious dementia. Stuck in a surreal landscape of constantly shifting emotions. No weight. Floating at the distant end of a tunnel. Miserably alone. Frightened. Voices growing louder, closing in. Wave after wave of depression. Needing to get high. Real high.

No more dope.

Unsure what to do, I panicked.

"God, what do you want me to do?" I cried. "What do you want me to do?"

I didn't wait for a response.

"I'll show you," I said with the giddiness and relief of a certified madman. "I'll show you."

More laughter mixed with tears.

"I'm going to set myself on fire."

Hysteria.

"Then I'll be safe. Yeah, then I'll be okay."

Now here's how I really burned up. Usually, before I go to bed I have a little milk and cookies. One night I had that low-fat milk, that pasteurized shit, and I dipped my cookie in it and the shit blew up. And it scared the shit out of me. Not the blowing up, but the catching on fire.

Imagining relief was nearby, I reach for the cognac bottle on the table in front of me and poured it all over me. Real natural, methodical. As the liquid soiled my body and clothing, I wasn't scared. Neither did I feel inner peace.

I was in a place called There.

Suddenly, my isolation was interrupted by a knock on the door. A bang, really. My cousin opened it and looked inside at the moment I picked up my Bic lighter. I saw him trying to figure out what I was doing.

"Come on in," I said.

He zeroed in on the lighter in my hand.

"Oh no!" he exclaimed.

"Don't be afraid."

Then I flicked it. The lighter didn't work. I tried it again and nothing. Then I did it a third time.

WHOOSH!

I was engulfed in flame.

Have you ever burned up? It's weird. Because you go, "Hey, I'm not in the fireplace. I am fucking burning up!"

Instinctively, I jumped on the bed, thinking that I'd grab the comforter, wrap myself up, and smother the flames. But God's wonderful. That comforter was just laying on the bed, not tucked in or anything. But the damn comforter wouldn't come loose. Wouldn't let me pick it up or wrap it around. It wouldn't move an inch. It was just stuck.

"Ahhhhhhhhhhhhhhhhhhhhhhhhhhhh!" I screamed.

I was in a place that wasn't heaven or earth. I must've gone into shock because I didn't feel anything.

I sat on the floor when my Aunt Dee rushed in. She peeked in the room as if she was scared of what she'd see. I motioned her to come in.

"Smother him!" she yelled to my cousin.

"What the fuck you talking about, smother him?" I said, though I don't know if any sound came out.

In my mind, I thought that "smother him" meant something bad. Like, "Put the sorry motherfucker out of his misery."

Still on fire—though unaware that I'd turned into a human barbecue—I rubbed the back of my head and looked at my hand. Flames rose from my skin. Scared the shit out of me. I screamed, "What the fuck is that?"

"You're on fire," my auntie exclaimed, and then to my cousin she barked, "Put a sheet over him."

Again, in my delusion, I thought that they wanted to kill me. Taking advantage of their confusion and horror, I leaped up and jumped out the window. That really took them by surprise. Sprinting down the driveway, I went out the gates, and ran down the street.

"Come back here, honey!" my auntie called.

But I kept going. Running, running down Parthenia. I was out of my mind.

Catching on fire is inspiring. They should use it for the Olympics. 'Cause I did the hundred-yard dash in about 4.6 in the underbrush.

There was a lot of traffic on Parthenia. I saw people looking at me, you know, and I couldn't understand what they were looking at. It felt like a parade. I wondered if I was missing something good. But they were looking at a man burning up.

And you know something I noticed? When you run down the street on fire, people will move out of your way. They don't fuck around. They get the fuck out of your way. Except for one old drunk who's sitting there going, "Hey, buddy, can I get a light? Come on, pal. A little off the sleeve?"

By the time I hit Hayvenhurst, my pace had slowed to a walk. A police car pulled up. Two cops tried to help me. I tried reaching for one of their guns. They could've blown my fucking head off. I wanted them to shoot me. Hoped they'd finish what I'd already started.

But I had no fight in me. My hands and face were already swollen. My clothes in burnt tatters. And my smoldering chest smelled like a burned piece of meat. They held me as an ambulance pulled up and helped get me inside.

"Oh, Lord, you got me now," I muttered.

Then my Aunt Dee, out of breath, bless her heart, got there. She climbed in and started talking to the ambulance attendant. More conversation I couldn't understand as they began treatment for my burns by covering me with a fluid-treated sheet.

The siren wailed.

"Is there?" I asked.

"Is there what?" someone asked.

"Oh, Lord, there is no help for a poor widow's son, is there?"

27

AT THE SHERMAN OAKS COMMUNITY HOSPITAL BURN CENTER: "Do you know who I am?" the man in the white coat asked me. "I said, 'Do you know who I am?'"

"Yeah," I said. "You're the doctor."

In the background, I heard people whispering that I'd fucked up. That I'd fucked up royally.

You can tell when you've fucked up because the doctor goes, "Holy shit! Why don't we just get some coleslaw and serve this up?"

They wrapped me in cloth shit. I complained that it felt tight. The pain was so bad I turned numb.

"You're going to touch me first. Then I'm going to die?"

The Burn Center's waiting room turned into a circus of the most concerned. My family filled the place. Aunt Dee, Uncle Dickie, Maxine, and Shelley. My kids also came in case they needed to pay their last respects.

Some in the group couldn't wait for the outcome. They simply went back to Northridge and picked the house clean of jewelry, televisions, and shit.

But that family shit was kid's stuff compared to the way God was torturing me for having transformed myself into a human torch. Physically, I was scarred from the tip of my ears down to my thighs. The most severe damage was concentrated on my upper body, where third-degree burns turned what was once smooth, unmarked, brown skin into a raw, fleshy paste that oozed brown pus and left the nerves exposed.

Emotionally, I didn't know which way was up. I have only vague images of: calling my agent and asking him to get me the hell out. An orderly asking for an autograph. Not permitting Jennifer to visit—my way of punishing her for God only knew what. Probably for getting clean. Jim Brown guarding the door. Deboragh wincing at the sight of me.

To be sure, I had the look of something created by a Hollywood special effects department. Wrapped in gauze. Slimy stuff dripping down my face. Moans coming out of my mouth.

But little registered with me other than the sheer, ceaseless pain. The intensity was punishing. It drove me in and out of consciousness. I conversed with God, pleading, cajoling, trying my best to get his attention.

Finally, I heard him respond: "Richard, this fire is too much. I'm going to relieve you for now. I'll call you later."

He kept his word, too. One day the male nurse who cared for me—a big black man with incredible patience and kindness—entered my room holding a sponge for me to see. He showed me both sides—one soft, the other full of little bristles. Didn't look like much. And the way he described it to me, in a real slow, even voice, made me feel like a kindergartner.

This guy Larry Murphy would come in and he kept talking to me every day. He said, "Now we gonna wash you pretty soon and put you in the tub."

I said, "Yeah, man, goddamn."

And he said, "And we gonna wash you."

"This—is—a—sponge, and—I—am—going—to—wash—your—back," he said.

"Okay," I said.

"And—it's—going—to—hurt."

"Ain't going to hurt me, man," I said.

One day I said, "Motherfucker, put me in the tub. I don't want to hear this shit anymore. Just wash my ass, please."

So they put me in this tub and he said, "How do you feel?"

After some preparation, he ran it across my back and I swear to God I screamed like a baby. Can't even describe that pain. Shitfuckmotherfuckerohgoddamnshitohfuckgodhelpmefuckfuckfuckfuck doesn't even come close

"Don't touch another motherfucking thing on me! I'm getting up and walking out. I don't care if I die, but you ain't gonna touch me with that motherfucking sponge. Please, don't touch me with that stuff.

After receiving this treatment twice a day for four weeks, a nurse mentioned that they weren't authorized to give me painkillers, but if I asked for them—

"I've been here all this time and you're just now telling me that all I have to do is ask?" I said incredulously.

"Yes, Mr. Pryor."

I went right back to my room, buzzed my doctor, and told him that I wanted painkillers. I watched as the nurse injected Demerol in my IV. Moments later, the most throbbing pain I'd ever felt melted into thin air. It was like a pleasant little hum overtook my entire being, brain and body, and I understood the nod of heroin addicts. They go for that hum.

Between the scrubbing and the skin grafts that initiated the long, painful healing process, I had no doubt of the horror story I created. Toward the end of my hospital say, I also began talking with a therapist, who tried addressing the problems and feelings that led to my suicide attempt. This psychiatrist got right to business. Made me talk about my ma, my grandmother, my father, the neighborhood where I grew up.

I cried like a baby and I wasn't even being scrubbed.

◆   ◆   ◆

The toxicity level of my blood was so high from the amount of drugs I'd done prior to the accident that doctors erroneously thought I must've been sneaking coke into the hospital. They questioned me daily. During that time, though, the only drug I had—other than what was prescribed by doctors—was television. Every Sunday, I watched the religious shows. Those televangelists became my new addiction.

They were so obviously full of shit, hustling the poor in the name of God, that I started imagining what would happen if Jesus himself surprised one of those charlatans by walking into the picture and tapping him on the shoulder, you know?

"Well, hi, Jesus. I was just talking about what you said in—"

"Said what? In where? Man, what are you talking about? I can't even write. Don't know how to spell. What are you talking about?"

"Well, you know that you said you were so and so—"

"Man, I didn't say none of it. I didn't say any of that stuff in that book. But here I am."

"Hallelujah."

"Yeah, thought I'd visit the United States. I hear and see so much. You all say so much about me. Put so many things in my mouth. Make me out to be different, like I give special concessions for special people and so forth. But my law is my law, no exceptions."

"Amen."

"Don't know what you're so happy about, brother. In any case, as long as I'm here, there're just a few people I'd like to say hello to. Like I remember there was a guy who had this dream that one day people of all colors … Ring a bell?"

"Martin Luther King, Jr."

"Yeah. Good guy. I'd like to say hello."

"He was killed. Assassinated."

"What? I don't believe it."

"God bless his soul."

"You leave my Father out of this. Now how about this leader you people used to have. Man said something about not what the country could do for you but what you could do for … I'd just like to have a quick word with him."

"He was also assassinated."

"I don't believe you people. I also know of some children, little children, who said their prayers every night. I loved hearing them pray. Such good kids. Little voices sounded like music. I'd just like to say goodbye to them."

"I'm sorry."

"Them, too? Just because they were different colors?"

"I'm afraid so."

"I'll give you something to be afraid of, Jack. I mean, how can you mess up so badly. How can you just destroy love? My Father gave you this world, and I gave you love. If you mess that up, too, I hope somebody will have mercy on you because I certainly won't."

"Thank you, Jesus. Now people, how can you resist a heartfelt plea like that? Please, send in whatever you can—ten dollars, twenty dollars, fifty dollars. We have payment plans..."

Going home was a relief. Buoyed by 25,000 letters from well-wishers and an army of visitors, I settled into the slow, painstaking, and painful routine of recovery. Basically, that consisted of taking baths and rubbing salves into my skin. At night I slept in a corset that was supposed to prevent my grafts from shrinking. I was also supposed to try not to scratch, but my fingernails scraped the soft, itchy skin until I drew blood.

In my state, pleasure and pain were the same. I was fortunate to have survived my fiery accident, but after the doctors, treatments, and pills were all done, I was still afflicted with the same old problems, fears, and pains that had caused me to drink a bottle of vodka a day, spend upward of $250,000 a year on cocaine, beat women, and then work to make them love me again.

The scars I now had on the outside only mirrored the ones I'd had on the inside my entire life.

Naturally, I got hung up on the superficial. I didn't think I could ever let a woman see me again, you know? That was something basic. Something immediate. For a while there, I flashed on the Great Pussy Drought of the 1980s and, brother, it was a frightening thought.

If I couldn't fuck no more, then what, you know?

I was wrong, though. Deboragh, bless her heart, was my first woman after the accident.

After the fire, a lot of people said, "God was punishing you." No, if God wanted to punish my ass, he would've burned my dick. When the fire hit, my dick went to work. "Emergency! Piss, come—do something! Don't let the fire get to the balls!"

And my chest was hollering, "Help!"

My dick said, "Fuck you. Every man for himself. Spit! I'm protecting the balls."

With Deboragh, it was like I'd never done it before. But then oh, God, did I do it, you know? It was beautiful.

I felt myself fall in love.

With Deboragh. Always with Deboragh.

But also with life.

I saw it all—the brightness that starts the day, makes the flowers, causes a hobo to smile, and inspires a woman to sing. It was right there, man.

Life.

As bright as the fucking sun.

I rubbed it all over my damn face.

And for that moment, it was mine and I was glad to be alive.

28

I'D NEVER BEEN HIGHER THAN I WAS IN HAWAII ONE DAY TOWARD the end of 1980. After ten hours' worth of flying lessons, I took over the controls of my single-engine Grumman Tiger and piloted the plane myself from Oahu to Maui. It was a transcendental moment. My whole life I'd wanted to fly. As a kid, I'd told one of my teachers about my dream and he'd laughed at me. I could still hear him say, "Richard, you can't do that."

Yet at age forty, I was doing just that. Likewise, plenty of people doubted whether I'd be able to refrain from my self-destructive ways. Privately, I was among them. But as I soared above the lush, emerald green island, banking to the right, then to the left, and then slowly circling the island's crystal blue perimeter, I was overwhelmed by the freedom of being above it all, and I felt as if I could prove them wrong, too.

Any doubts I had about how the public would react following the accident were quickly erased. After its December release, *Stir Crazy* went on a tear at the box office, grossing more than $100 million. In April, the Hollywood community showed their support with a standing ovation when I presented an Oscar at the Academy Awards. Then *Bustin' Loose*, which I finished after recovering from my burns, continued my winning streak that summer.

In Hawaii, the high life was replaced by a healthy, isolated life in Hana. I retreated into the slow lane of my newly completed, modern, Japanese-style home, which was situated on a hill overlooking five plush, gorgeously landscaped acres of flowers and trees. Every room had its own deck. I looked outside, into the gardens and then out beyond, to the ocean, and one word came to mind:

Yes.

But fruit juices, jogging, and shoji doors didn't ensure life would be as sweet as the orchids in my garden. The affection I craved was still damn elusive. I tried Deboragh. I dallied with a Korean actress. I coerced my cute Japanese maid in Hawaii. I pretty-pleased Jennifer back into my life. I tried all thirty-one flavors, whatever I felt like at the time but when it came to womens, relationships, trying to satisfy the urge to get loved, I couldn't find the right prescription.

It's not that I lacked for love, but what I was able to feel was as momentary as the high I got sucking on the pipe. My therapist plumbed my childhood for reasons. Motherfucker made some points that were hard to accept. But true.

"That's why life stinks," I said.

"What do you mean?"

"To me, this life stinks because all we want is love," I went on. "That's all anybody wants. Black, white, orange. Race, nationality, none of that shit matters. We're all human beings and we all want love. That's all."

"I think you're right," he said. "How does that make life stink?"

"Because the motherfucker's fleeting, you know? It won't stay put."

Was that the problem, Rich?

Or was it that you didn't love yourself?

◆   ◆   ◆

In February 1981, I returned to the mainland to prepare for work on *Some Kind of Hero*. Drug-free until then, my Northridge home was filled with the ghosts of when I wasn't clean. They'd waited around like ghoulish fans for my homecoming, but instead of wanting my autograph, they asked, "When we gonna smoke, Rich? When we gonna get high, man?"

The big house had been vacuumed and cleaned of all my old drug paraphernalia eight months earlier. The day of my accident the stuff had been thrown out. Not on account of me. No, nobody wanted the police to find it. But as soon as I walked inside that place, I knew there was some shit around. I sensed it. Sniffed it like a bloodhound.

After waiting till the house was quiet and I was alone, I went to where I kept my supersecret stash. A little drawer. Lo and behold, I had the exhilarating rush of a prospector who pans the river, sifts through the silt, looks down, and sees a golden nugget sparkling in the sunlight.

Eureka!

There was a little rock.

One perfect little rock.

I picked it up and marveled at its whiteness. Brightness. A star in the night sky.

Make a wish, Rich.

A few minutes later, I found a glass pipe.

Locked in my bedroom, I flicked my Bic for the first time since the fire.

"Oh, Jesus," I sighed as the rush began. "Oh, God."

Though I appeared to be in fine form as *Some Kind of Hero* filmed that summer, I'd climbed aboard the old self-destructive roller coaster without anybody knowing it. I wanted so badly to prove that I was the same old Richard Pryor that I actually became him. I kept a tiny pipe in my trailer and got loaded whenever I could get my hands on some coke. By August, I was back in the same rut.

So was my personal life. My six-month affair with *Hero* co-star Margot Kidder ended just before the movie did, when she discovered that I was cheating on her. She didn't get mad—much. But she got even by coming over to the hotel where I'd taken up permanent residence and scissoring the Armani wardrobe hanging in my closet.

Thank God that's all she cut.

In the meantime, I repaired old ties. Before *Hero* ended, I'd proposed to Jennifer. It took three tries, including a final proposal at a pool party in Hana where I smoked some Maui Wowie pot that was as powerful as an LSD trip, before she finally accepted.

Our marriage took place in a backyard ceremony on August 16, 1982, and Jenny looked resplendent in white and flowers, but the evening was short on celebration. As for a reception, Margot sent an angry telegram. My pretty Japanese maid, who'd taken to keeping a bottle of vodka by the Mr. Clean—using one to mop and the other to mope—got sloppy drunk and cried that she was losing me. And in the morning, having sobered up, I called my attorney in L.A. and asked him to get the damn marriage annulled.

"I woke up and realized what I'd done," I explained. "I said, 'Shit, I don't want to be married.'"

By October, I had initiated preliminary divorce proceedings, slept with other women, and physically pummeled Jennifer, but something in me couldn't let go completely. Pressured into making another concert film, which I wasn't ready to do, I knew instinctively that I had to hang on to Jenny in some way, shape, or form. She'd gone through it with me before.

"You aren't ready," she counseled. "Don't do it."

"But they're telling me that I have to cash in," I countered. "They say now's my time. Now's my time."

But December came and I knew it wasn't time. Rather than work out for weeks and then tour, honing each routine to a razor sharpness, as I did before the first concert picture in 1979, I went up to Oakland the week before we filmed and fucked up. Too much booze, too much coke. I was little better when I got in front of the camera the first night at the Hollywood Palladium.

In a scene reminiscent of my breakdown in Las Vegas fifteen years earlier, I asked myself, "What the fuck am I doing here?"

Then I walked off stage.

Over the next couple days, I delivered the goods, enough so that producer Ray Stark, agent Guy McElwaine, and other powers behind the movie were mostly satisfied, but all of them knew they'd need to reshoot parts. As for me, I split for Hawaii. Told Jennifer, "They made the gentle mistake of giving me the money in advance. Bye-bye."

"They didn't give you all the money," she said.

"Yes they did," I said, flashing an evil smile.

Eventually, I finished the live-concert film by performing at what was essentially an invitation-only party, but after the footage was spliced with the Palladium bits, it still played as inspired, cutting-edge theater. Even so, *Live on the Sunset Strip* wasn't as great an overall performance as the first concert picture, but with routines like "Mafia Club," "Africa," and "Freebase," it had its moments.

And, fortunately, so did I.

It's nice to be able to laugh later.
I thank you for all the love you sent me, and I mean that sincerely.

Offstage, I was not nearly as sentimental. In January 1982, I embarked on Jennifer's and my belated honeymoon, a cruise through the Caribbean. If we hadn't been fighting at the time of departure, she would also have been on board the *Silver Trident*, the luxury yacht I'd leased for the occasion. In her place I found other female amusement when I wasn't too fucked up.

But I missed her terribly, and after ten days of ship-to-shore, me sweet-talking and pleading from such appropriately romantic-sounding locales as Teardrop Cove, she succumbed to the lure of our mad addiction to each other.

It may not have been a traditional honeymoon, but there was no mistaking it as anything but ours. Wild and woolly, we were George and Martha sailing across the high seas of love. Passionate lovemaking spoiled by drinking and fighting. After less than two weeks, she jumped ship and got a divorce lawyer, and I finished up the vacation with another woman.

As always, Dr. Jekyll's good intentions were fucked up by Mr. Hyde. The shit was beyond my control. I couldn't escape the darkness.

Late on the night of March 4, 1982, John Belushi, Robin Williams, and Robert De Niro had come by the Comedy Store looking for me to participate in their wee-hours carousing. Luckily, I happened not to be there. Otherwise I might have—and to my mind, probably would have—ended up going back to the Chateau Marmont and doing cocaine with Belushi, who died early on March 5.

It could easily have been me.

I was just as lucky in cheating death a month and a half later when I worked on *The Toy* with Jackie Gleason in Baton Rouge, Louisiana. I didn't much care for the picture. Like the others, I did it for the monies. But Jackie and I hit it off famously, like kindred souls.

The shit Jackie talked between setups was funnier than anything we got in the movie. He knew about gangsters, gamblers, comics, vaudeville, strippers, and sharks. He'd start talking about something that happened in the 1970s and then suddenly he'd be swirling around the 1920s and '30s, describing people and joints so good I could smell them.

One day he asked me to get him some grass. I found some and gave it to him on the bench where we used to sit and talk. It overlooked a lake that had no fish in it. But Jackie didn't like the way I handed it to him. He showed me a sneaky way of handling the exchange, and then he winked.

"That's called a switch," he said.

We laughed. Two stars. Getting paid a few million dollars. And we were practicing dope deals.

Goddamn, that was funny to me.

Then things got serious. One day I felt my heart pound in rebellion to my secret dalliances with the evil white lady. An ambulance rushed me to a New Orleans hospital. I really thought I might actually die right then, and the only thing that really bothered me about it was being in the South. Down there, people didn't care if a black man died. Or else the Klan would be so glad they'd declare a holiday.

Otherwise, I figured the rest of my family had gone. Maybe it was my time, you know?

But it turned out to be a warning. According to the doctors, it was my Wolff-Parkinson-White syndrome acting up, a sudden arrhythmia, which they could treat. I explained that the palpitations had come during a scene I shot in a swamp opposite a live alligator. The gator had said, "Ah, blackened catfish." With that, my heart began sprinting for shore.

It didn't know the rest of me couldn't swim.

Deep down, I knew the truth. Lying in my hospital bed, I let my mind wander back to the time when I'd asked Redd Foxx why I always wanted more, more, more cocaine, and how he'd looked at my ignorant face and told me it was because I was an addict.

An addict.

I didn't tell anyone.

As if it was a secret. As if it wasn't true.

But who were you fooling, Rich?

Even then you wanted more.

29

YES, I WAS UNREPENTANT, EVEN WITH THAT SCARE, AS I WENT off to London to play the villain in *Superman III*. And yes, the movie was a piece of shit. But even before I read the script, the producers offered me $4 million, more than any black actor had ever been paid.

"For a piece of shit," I'd told my agent when I finally read the script, "it smells great."

But the money couldn't buy what I needed. One night Margot Kidder stopped by my room to see if I'd go out with her. She observed me sitting in the middle of the floor of a vast, luxurious suite, sucking on a crack pipe. I was surrounded by empty vials.

She muttered something about me being such a sad sight.

So fucking sad.

What could I say?

"What did you say, Rich?"

"Nothing. I just kept smoking."

There were moments when I dreamed of escaping my misery just as I had before I'd set myself on fire. I just couldn't find an escape that suited me. I took my kids to Hana for Christmas, making a big show of it though in truth it was nothing more than an empty gesture. I wasn't capable of anything else.

Remember when Rain stood in the doorway. She and the others were going to the beach.

"Daddy, come with us," she said. "Come on."

I was grouchy and hungover. I looked out at the beautiful Hawaiian afternoon, sunny and warm. The blue Pacific glistened in the distance like a sapphire I might've given a woman after having the guilties for cheating on her. None of it registered with me.

I wanted the kids to go already.

But they wanted their dad.

So?

That's what I thought.

I just wanted to do my base.

Then the strangest thing happened. Left alone, I asked myself what I was doing. You know? In a moment of clarity, I glimpsed the absolute pitifulness of my situation. Got a clear view through the window of hopelessness and despair.

You go through changes in your life and you just fucking change. Something happened in my life that just fucking changed my mind about all the shit. I used to think I knew everything, man. I'd be fucked up and I knew it. I knew all the shit.

And all of a sudden I didn't know shit.

I was one of the dumbest motherfuckers that ever lived. If you catch me on the wrong day and ask me my name, you're gonna get trouble.

"How'd you end up like that again, Rich?"

Although the answer was in my heart, I dealt with what was in my hands. Trembling but determined, I tossed the shit in the garbage. For real. No hiding the pipe in one drawer and the rock in another and tiptoeing away for a few minutes. I chucked it. Grabbing my cigarettes, I walked to the beach. As I shuffled onto the sand, my kids looked as if they saw an alien.

In a way, they did.

"Daddy!"

Even I was tempted to turn around and look at who they were talking about.

"Daddy!"

But then it was great. Rain taught me how to float. Bobbing in the salty water, I got into the sensation of buoyancy, the feeling of levitating off the ground. I imagined drifting away from my addiction, away from the dark rooms where I was prisoner to the pipe. Staring up at the sky, I saw the immensity of the spinning world. The gulls squawked. My kids squawked. The water slapped the shore.

Like music.

And I was in the middle of it.

Alive.

And grateful to be there, you know?

Several weeks later, I got a call from a friend. Coincidentally, she'd checked herself into rehab and wanted me to help her in recovery by participating in therapy. Ordinarily, I would've told her "no". In my neighborhood, the administration of affection had always been a one-way street. However, in my newfound sobriety I asked where and when and hopped on a place.

Although there was no bigger skeptic than me, the therapy sessions had an unanticipated effect on me. I listened in the group meetings, where people stood up and told harrowing stories caused by their addictions. I thought back to when I was seven and my grandmother took me to an evangelist in Springfield and pleaded with him to rid me of the devil.

Even then I thought that shit was funny.

But now I heard things that sounded too familiar to laugh off. Gradually, I recognized the picture being assembled by these confessions was of me.

I had to quit drinking. I got tired of waking up in my car driving ninety. You know? Trying to talk to the police when your mouth won't work.

One day, caught in the fervor, I stood up and admitted that I, too, was a drug addict and alcoholic.

It wasn't anything I didn't know already.

Amen.

Or hadn't known for many years.

Sing it, brother.

But to say it out loud, in front of strangers, without adding a punch line, man, that was like saying adios to the greatest, funniest character I'd ever created.

My best work, you know. And it scared the hell out of me.

Hallelujah!

"I know you, motherfucker," I said. "We ran for a long time. But I'm tired of you hurting me. Let's declare a truce. Leave each other alone. See how it goes, you know?"

No response.

"Okay?"

No response.

"Please?"

"We'll see. If you just shut up."

Even sober, I couldn't control my addiction to the womens. Deboragh started out by my side when I began a lengthy spring tour in preparation for another live-concert film. But after a performance in Washington, D.C., I met twenty-year-old Flynn Be-Laine. Within two days, I shuffled Debbie off to Buffalo, so to speak, and cozied up to Flynn.

By any standards, Flynn was drop-dead fine. Strong legs, nice breasts, and sweet smile.

I was like a mouse sniffing around a trap.

But it was good, you know?

There were other womens, too. A Julie in New Orleans, where I filmed most of *Here and Now.*

But when I added the finishing touches to the film in New York I had Flynn meet me there. Then I set her up in L.A. By August, though, I lost interest in her and went back to Jennifer. Naughty me. I couldn't help myself, and neither could she.

Flynn, bless her, was tough. She didn't give up. I wanted nothing to do with her, but she had other ideas. One day Jennifer slipped into my Rolls and saw a pair of baby booties hanging from the rearview mirror. Her eyes rolled.

"Flynn sent 'em," I said.

"You know what she's telling you, right?" Jenny asked.

Indeed. In February 1984, right before I received the Black Filmmaker's Hall of Fame Award, Flynn broke the news: She was pregnant. Clearly, I was a productive motherfucker, deserving of some Hall of Fame. But instead of celebrating Flynn's announcement, I ran to Deboragh, seeking consolation, advice, excuses. Seeking something. She knew as well as I did that my own need for parenting far exceeded my ability to be one.

My life's sentence, you know?

But that poor-pitiful-me-shit didn't play in Peoria, and it sure didn't play on Debbie's doorstep.

"Well, what am I supposed to do about it?" Debbie asked. "I didn't get her pregnant."

"I've got to do the right thing," I said.

For some reason, I thought I saw the pieces of my life falling into place much like a puzzle. Events took on a pattern and meaning. Such nonsense began making a certain amount of sense. I don't know why.

Following my accident, I had tried to write my autobiography but never quite got a grip on the three-hundred-pound alligator that was my life. Still too close to the fire. Didn't have perspective. I kept at it, though. Thinking about shit. Writing down bits and pieces, thoughts and shit.

Finally, I asked Mooney and Rocco Urbisci, a writer friend, to help me stitch it all together, and the result was *Jo Jo Dancer, Your Life is Calling*. Originally, I intended it to be a straight-out comedy, but I couldn't keep the sadness and emotion from spilling onto the page. It was beyond me, you know? Like therapy. I went with it.

Maybe a documentary would've played better. It would've had the edge of my standup. More dick, less heart. Or maybe more heart and less dick. I don't know.

I never will, either.

Jo Jo was the latest and biggest project my company, Indigo Productions, produced as part of a $40 million deal with Columbia Pictures. For my money—which it was—Indigo was a fiasco, something much bigger than I could handle. I didn't know how to run a company, and, come to think of it, I didn't even want a company, you know?

Jim Brown did, though.

I made my friend Jim president.

At the end of 1983 I fired him and all hell came down on top of me.

Jim, a complex man, liked running that company more than I liked having it. He hired lots of people. He made lots of noise. He commissioned numerous scripts. Started up all sorts of projects.

However, I wasn't happy about where the company was going. The only thing I cared about was the work, and when I sat down to read the scripts that had been developed, I couldn't find one that stood out as special. Not one screamed to be made, you know? I had to ask myself a serious question, something I tried my damnedest to avoid.

"Rich, do you want the company?"

"No."

And that's basically what I decided to tell Jim when I fired him.

I caught shit, though. The black film community was outraged. The NAACP turned on me. Everybody, it seemed to me, acted like it was my obligation to employ people just because of their skin color. They didn't understand. I didn't want to employ anybody— black, white, or purple.

I didn't give a shit anymore.

Jo Jo was the exception. The project was my own creation, my own madness. Certainly, it takes a degree of madness to produce, direct, co-write, and star in a movie. By the time I took all that damn film in the editing bay, I felt like a snake charmer slowly being strangled by his own charming pet viper. I just wanted to know how I might've fucked up. Not that I could see anything wrong. I was too close, and everyone around me only said how brilliant it was.

"Genius, Rich, that's what it is."

All that shit.

But goddamn it, I knew better. I just wanted someone to tell me where the holes were, you know?

"Right there," the doctor said. "Look there."

Flynn's legs were apart. My eyes were riveted to that amazing sight: my son Steven entering the world. On November 16, 1984, I actually stood in the delivery room and watched him being born, and now I can finally say it:

I'm glad I was sober.

If you've never seen a baby born, you ain't seen shit. I know if men had to push babies out their asshole, there'd be no question about abortion. Not even a smither of a question.

I saw this woman who I loved lying on a table with her legs open, a baby coming out of her pussy, and she had a smile on her face. Right then I knew she was crazy. That was proof.

I was just praying to God that the baby didn't come out and grab her hemorrhoids.

Then he came out, and that made me realize women have been bullshitting us. You know when you're fucking, really working, doing some serious damage, and she says, "It hurts." Well, if your dick is not as big around as my thigh, you ain't hurting shit, okay? I saw a baby, a whole entire human being, come out of this lady's pussy.

The doctor let me help pull him out. It was my baby boy, you know? And you hold it in your arms and do the stupidest shit. While she was recovering from the pain and the blood and shit, I took that little guy and held him up in the air. Like, "Behold the only man greater than myself!"

Then the doctor says, "Can you give him back to the mother so she can feed him?"

"No, motherfucker, I'm not finished beholding yet."

I still refused to marry Flynn and it cost me. I came back from a gambling binge in Las Vegas. Had my winnings in a briefcase.

Some $600,000 I'd won at the blackjack table. Flynn's lawyer was the first to congratulate me.

"That's about how much she'll need to take care of the boy," he said.

But that's life sometimes.

A simple, unpredictable roll of the dice.

PART 3

Mudbone,
part three

NOW SOMETHIN'S OBVIOUS TO ME. THESE HERE TIMES WE LIVE IN are tryin' times. But ya know what? Ain't never been no time when folks didn't have to try.

Shit, ya gotta try.

Every day ya gotta try'n get your lazy ass out of bed in the mornin'. Ya gotta try'n get somethin' to eat. Somethin' to drink. Try'n get a little pussy now and then.

Now Rich, he had spunk. He had a heart attack and then went on TV and said he could still make love nine or ten times a day. Absolutely knew he could. All he had to do was meet a woman and then he'd prove it.

'Cept it was a cover-up.

Boy was suffering.

Worn out. I know'd he was tired.

Loss of nerve. Maybe.

Bad breaks. For sure.

Not long after his movie came out, people were talking 'bout how he'd changed. Looked skinny and sickly.

People started talkin' it was AIDS 'n' shit. Thought never crossed my mind.

'Cause I know human nature.

Truth is, you lock yourself in a dark room and breathe that devil's snot every day, you gonna miss all the sunshine. Naturally, you gonna be miserable, quit tryin', give the sickness space to rent. Flower don't get sunshine, it ain't gonna grow. People don't get enough sunshine, they ain't gonna see any reason to try'n bloom, either.

Reminds me of a fella I knew named Black-Eye Titus.

Shit, you probably never heard of old Black-Eye. But I knew him well. Heard of him long before I met him, but that's 'cause Black-Eye was famous. Famous the same way ol' Josh Gibson and Buck O'Neil were famous baseball players. White folks ignored them 'cause they were black, but Josh and Buck knew they were among the greatest who ever played the game.

Same with Black-Eye. He was the greatest entertainer I ever saw, and that includes a lady I once knew in Paris. She could whistle Dixie without using her mouth, if you get my drift. But that's besides the point.

A great dancer 'n' singer, Black-Eye came along at a time, way back in the 1910s and '20s, when not much notice was given to black performers like him. People too busy payin' attention to Al Jolson, who was okay if you liked schizophrenics. But I never much understood that blackface shit.

Course, Black-Eye noticed what was goin' on with Jolson and got the notion of rubbing white shit over his face. Only thing you'd be able to see were his black eyes—the reason for his name. Black folks loved his ass, though. Paid him just for walkin' down 125th Street, and that was after his show. And those white folks who saw him left dazzled.

He had a chance to go as big as Jolson.

Maybe bigger. But that's what scared folks.

One night when he was asleep in his car—had to sleep in his car 'cause no hotel'd give him a room—some motherfucking Klansmen snuck up and cut off his legs. Laughed that he was no man no more. He was half a man. Exactly how they considered black people in general.

I was supposed to see Black-Eye perform that next night. Had a pretty little girl. But the curtain went up and a kid named Callaway came on. Nothin' was ever said 'bout Black-Eye and no one heard of him again.

◆   ◆   ◆

'BOUT *forty-somethin' years later, I was passin' through Peoria, Illinois, and wandered into Collins' Corner, a little black 'n' tan joint in town, where I was supposed to see a young performer. There happened to be an old man at the piano, playin' 'n' singin' and smilin' at some of the ladies. The fat ones. And I didn't think nothin' much of it, 'cept that I liked the way he sang.*

Then I got up to meet a pretty thing. That's when I noticed the old man was in a wheelchair.

Upon closer inspection, I saw he didn't have no legs.

Well, I put one and one together, and sure enough it was two. Black-Eye Titus was still alive and kickin', so to speak.

"Was down 'n' out for a spell," he explained.

"You was the greatest," I said. "What happened?"

"It's this way," he said. "I never much noticed my legs was gone as much as I did my spirit. If I couldn't dance—because that's what I did best—then I figured I couldn't do nothing. 'Sides, when I didn't have my face, nobody knew I was Black-Eye, including me."

"You mean without the cream..."

"Yep. Without the cream, there was no coffee."

We probably would've kept talkin' if Bris Collins, the club's owner, hadn't told us to shut up or get out. As it happened, he introduced a young singer-comedian named Richard Pryor, which was the whole reason I was there anyway. Passing through town just to give him some advice.

I wished I woulda told him 'bout Black-Eye. 'Cause before we quit talkin', ol' Black-Eye told me how he spent years tryin' to drink himself to death. One night he figured he was on his way to doin' just that. And when he opened his eyes in the mornin', it was because he felt something warm on his face, and it felt mighty good.

"Turned out it was just the sun," he chuckled.

"And that was enough?" I asked.

"Well, the thought dawned on me that it could be. A little pussy, a little warmth. Same thing. It's like God's up there playin' craps, and all of us peoples is just one roll of the dice. You ain't gonna be a seven every day, but you can hope, and most times that's enough for me."

30

AS A REWARD FOR *JO JO*, I DECIDED TO SPRINT ACROSS THE country in my Ferrari. People asked why. Simply because I had a Testarossa, you know. That was reason enough. Going 130 miles an hour, I wanted to blaze my own path into the future. Slip in and out of time as it applied to people. Flee the past. Escape Hollywood, a town I didn't like in the first place.

But where were you going, Rich?

I didn't know.

I was just going. Going fast, too.

But where?

Maybe nowhere. Maybe just away.

Or maybe I was trapped.

Trapped in a cosmic joke, you know?

If so, I wasn't alone. Geraldine Mason, a pretty actress who'd auditioned for *Jo Jo*, sat beside me. She had stars for eyes, a smile as bright as a sign in front of the hotel in Las Vegas where we partied for a few days, and, as far as I knew, she really wanted to be with me.

We sped through Las Vegas, intent on getting to Peoria in record time. Somewhere along the way, Geraldine mentioned she might be pregnant. I didn't know there was such a condition as "might be pregnant."

"Maybe we'll get lucky," she said softly. "Maybe nothing will happen."

In my entire life nothing was something that never happened to me, and that didn't change in 1986.

That summer the first signs of a serious problem surfaced. It snuck up on me while I finished shooting *Critical Condition* in L.A. I remember being tired by that time, feeling drained of my normal energy. Then one day the floor caved in. I had been resting in a chair between set-ups and camera changes when director Michael Apted finally asked me to take my place.

I heard him loud and clear.

No problem.

"Okay, Michael," I said.

The message was relayed to my brain.

My brain said, You have to get the fuck up, Rich.

But nothing moved.

Raise your ass up off the chair, my brain continued.

I tried. But nothing moved.

"Come on, Richard," the director said. "Quit fooling around."

I wasn't fooling around. That's what scared me.

"I'm not joking," I called. "I'm trying to get there."

And I was. Real hard. But my body wasn't buying that shit. It was fucking with me. Like ha-ha-ha, you know?

I saw my legs. Told them to get up and go. But the job order got lost around my waist. My legs were on vacation.

Numb and dumb.

I didn't panic. Probably because I didn't know what the fuck was going on. I had to believe it was just a strange muscle twitch. Something that was going to pass. After massaging my legs, I shuffled my feet in place, a tentative start up, and then, just as strangely as the motherfuckers had quit, they started back up again.

My brain was going nuts: You're under your own power. Good, Rich. But what the fuck is going on? Don't matter. Just don't fall.

I walked funny, but at least I made it to where I was supposed to be and did my scene without incident.

Afterward, I didn't know what to make of the problem. I hoped I could forget about it. Tried to, anyway.

But it sure tripped up my sanity, you know?

After I guested on "The Tonight Show," a short time later, people noticed a dramatic change in my appearance. I'd suffered a noticeable loss of weight. My body was spindly and my face looked thin and tired. Suddenly, the rumor mill overflowed with speculation that I had AIDS. I didn't know what the fuck was wrong with me, but blood tests proved it wasn't AIDS.

I tried ignoring my symptoms, but that became impossible. At a charity basketball game, I fell down while dribbling the ball. Nobody was around me. My legs just took a time-out. I went splat. I looked like a motherfucking clown, though it obviously wasn't funny. After resting, I finished the game. But the incident shook me up.

Frightened by the way my eyesight and balance came and went without informing me of its schedule, I finally saw my longtime physician. After he asked a ton of questions and performed numerous tests, I asked him what he thought might be the problem. He looked at me as if I'd just walked through the door.

"I'm not sure," he said.

Well, I knew that much. Motherfucker did everything but make lemonade from my piss and didn't know more than I did. That infuriated me, you know?

Because something was wrong.

"I don't believe you," I said.

My intuition told me that he suspected the problem, but didn't want to tell me. Conservative doctor shit.

"We need more information," he counseled. "I really think you should go to the Mayo Clinic for more tests."

It took until August for him to finally persuade me it was in my best interests to stop ignoring the problem and go for an examination. Childlike in my fear of what they might discover, I asked Debbie to accompany me. Though we hadn't spoken for a while, she agreed. In spite of all the reasons we couldn't live together, we still loved each other.

For the next week, I went through a series of intensive, often frightening and exhausting tests. Embarrassed when my eyes' inability to focus prevented me from describing pictures on large cards, I shifted into unrestrained terror when I saw the needle they were going to use during my spinal tap. At least the pretty nurse was nice.

"Now, Mr. Pryor, don't move," she said.

"I won't," I replied. "I'm looking at your titties."

The brief glimpse might've been the lone bright spot. Unable to handle the fear of what the doctors were going to find, I secretly turned to the only relief I'd ever known. One night Debbie, worried by the unusually long time I stayed in the bathroom, opened the door and caught me fumbling with a tourniquet and syringe as I shot up with Demerol.

Oh, Mama.

I stared at her, helpless and frightened and silent.

Mama.

She didn't say a word. She took in the scene and backed out of the room, shutting the door.

In the movies, I would've heard crying coming from the other side. But there was nothing.

Just the sound of my heart beating and the silent cry in my head for my mother to make it all better.

At the end of the week, Debbie and I finally met with the doc. For five days, I'd been asking what they thought and getting mystified shrugs in return. Now they had a diagnosis. In a plain, emotionless voice, the doctor told me that I had multiple sclerosis. Debbie and I turned and exchanged blank, worried looks.

Multiple sclerosis.

Those two words hit me like a ball on a backboard.

Bounce.

"Oh, I got it?" I said. "What is it?"

The doctor's face was all funny and shit. I'd never heard a doctor just say, "Ahhhhhhhhh."

"So what is it, doc?"

"Ahhhhhhhhhhhh."

"That means you don't know anything about this shit, right?"

"Ahhhhhhhhhhhh."

He told me that the MS was still in its infancy. That I was fortunate.

"Your prognosis is good, " he said. "Many people with MS can live for a long, long time. But…"

I told the doctor: "You don't know how the fuck I got it and you don't know when it's going away. So don't be bringing up theories about my cocaine. You didn't even know I did no cocaine."

He still said, "Maybe it was those two ounces you did that time."
I said, "Man, what do you mean, 'that time'? I did two ounces every time."
"Well, slow down."

I flew back to L.A. in shock. Neither Debbie nor I mentioned a word about MS the entire flight. I didn't know what to think. Living life so large, bigger than life, you tend to believe you have some sort of superhuman power. I'd left the ghetto behind. The whorehouses of my youth were like postcards from past journeys. I'd walked through fire. Seen my own motherfucking flesh regenerate. I wanted to see myself as a blessed motherfucker. But suddenly I felt the floor start wobbling. Like in an earthquake, my footing was unsure. All my different incarnations stared at me. Child, comedian, asshole, addict, man, father, husband, actor, victim, superstar, patient, child.

They all wanted to know the same thing.

"What now, motherfucker?"

It occurred to me then that at the outset of life God gives you a certain number of angels. They hover above you, protecting your ass from danger. But if you cross a certain line too many times, they get the hell away. Say, "Hey, motherfucker, you've abused us too many times. From here on, you're on your own."

That's what scared me—the prospect of being alone. One option was to marry Flynn. Despite all my philandering, she remained as determined as ever to become the next Mrs. Richard Pryor. She'd become a devout Jehovah's Witness, once even trying to convert me while sitting on the edge of my bed. But I didn't hold that against her any more than I did other shit.

Worn out and in deep denial, I caved in to fears of being alone, and on October 10, 1986, we married in a civil ceremony performed in a judge's chambers. She brought a girlfriend to witness the occasion; I didn't bring nothing but misgivings.

In the weeks following the wedding, I started working out new material at the Comedy Store. Some people talk to psychiatrists, but my biggest insights had always come onstage, so for me it was therapeutic. About the AIDS rumors, I said, "That was funny the first time I cleared out an elevator." Flynn's and my twenty-two-year age difference also proved fruitful. "My wife is young," I said. "The school bus had her back on time today."

But it just wasn't the same as before. My performance lacked the passion that had always given my performances an incendiary edge. After leaving the Mayo Clinic, the only constant was the level of chaos in my life. It reached the danger zone when Geraldine gave birth to my son Franklin. The news pissed off Flynn, who wanted to be the mother of the youngest Pryor offspring.

What could I do, you know?

Try—to—get—away!

If only I'd been able. Separated in early December—after less than two months of marriage—our divorce was finalized in January. As we left for court, Flynn sashayed out of the house wearing a fur coat with nothing on underneath.

The upshot?

Roughly ten months later, Kelsey was born.

She was my sixth child. Her mother was my fifth ex-wife.

I wondered if I was ever going to roll a seven. Probably not. Better not. Later on, I got a vasectomy to make sure I damn well didn't.

But God loves us all anyway, you know?

31

IN THE DREAM, I WAS STANDING OPPOSITE MY FATHER IN THE middle of a big field, throwing a baseball back and forth. For a long time, we played in silence, enjoying the warmth of the afternoon and the rhythm of the game. Then I started asking questions about my life. Mostly about my womens. Stupid shit. Like what he thought about Deboragh's ashtray. Did he like what Jennifer wore a particular night we went out. Shit like that.

As my arm tired, I asked if he knew that I'd gone to the Mayo Clinic and been diagnosed with MS. He caught the ball and threw it back. Suddenly, it seemed like a test.

"How do you feel, son?" he asked.

"Eh," I said with a shrug. "Sometimes better. Sometimes a little worse."

I threw the ball back and the game resumed. A while later, he interrupted the silence again.

"How do you feel, son?" he asked.

"Dad, if only I'd have known."

But the future doesn't let you know it's there until it bites you in the ass, particularly, as I discovered, when it includes multiple sclerosis. Chronic, disabling, and hard to detect, the disease attacks the central nervous system, destroying the protective casing that surrounds nerve fibers. Although rarely fatal, it produces symptoms that range from loss of coordination and muscle strength to mood shifts and depression —with some bladder weakness, memory loss, spasm, and even paralysis thrown in for good measure.

It was as if God had all this shit left over from the other afflictions he created and decided to throw it all into one disease. Kinda like a Saturday Surprise. It was a motherfucker. It ate you up from the inside out.

Instead of denial, I went into depression. By early 1988, I was hitting booze and pills pretty hard, spending a lot of time isolated in Hawaii. On a rare outing, I took Deboragh on a shopping spree to New York. While holed up at the Plaza Athénée, I snuck in a visit with Jennifer, who heard me ramble semicoherently about life and death and left thinking I was suicidal, though she never heard me reveal the reason why.

In August, I returned to Gotham City to star in *See No Evil, Hear No Evil*, another lackluster comedy reteaming me with Gene Wilder. My excuse was the money. I don't know what everybody else had in mind. Physically and emotionally, it was difficult to involve myself in the work. The picture also reunited me with Jennifer, who pestered me with questions about my distant, sullen, and markedly slower demeanor.

"Why are you walking like an old man?" she asked.

For weeks, I refused to answer. Why she didn't tire of such shit is testimony of our strange, twisted, and enduring love affair. Then one morning before I left for work, Jenny caught me unrolling my Comme des Garçons shirtsleeve over a thin stream of blood as I exited the bathroom. I'd just shot up.

"It's bunk," I said.

"Why, Richard?" she asked. "Why are you fucking with this shit again?"

The room was disturbingly silent for a long time before I was able to summon the courage to admit the last secret of my complicated life. But I don't think I could've said anything that would've shocked Jenny. We'd been through it all.

"I went to Mayo Clinic for some tests," I said. "I've been twice now."

"And?"

"I have multiple sclerosis."

"So that's the reason you're walking funny?"

"Yeah."

"And the bunk?"

No reply.

I had limits to what I thought needed explanations. I had my limits.

Even in the early stages, the disease was unpredictable. It came without warning, like a relative showing up unannounced at my doorstop. I'd get up to walk across the room, and while my mind would picture me striding as always, I'd actually be splattered on the floor, a fucked-up tangle of surprised arms and legs. I had no control. I'd look up and say, "God, it's in your hands."

I got a taste of things to come shortly after I moved from my longtime Northridge residence—it was more like fleeing the ghosts —into a two-story, Spanish-style house in Bel Air. Once I was walking up the long driveway when I lost control and fell down. Frightened, I called for help. The people who worked for me thought I was inside the house and ran up and down the stairs. About the time my fear turned into frustration, one of them finally poked her head out the front door and saw me waving like a castaway on a deserted island.

"There you are!" she exclaimed.

"Right," I said. "But you don't get no prize because of it."

It was like that, you know?

At the end of 1988, I worked on *Harlem Nights*, Eddie Murphy's pet movie project. At the time, no one was bigger. Exercising his clout, he was the picture's writer, director, and star. He was trying to scale the same mountain that I climbed making *Jo Jo*. I should've warned the motherfucker.

I never connected with Eddie. People talked about how my work had influenced Eddie, and perhaps it did. But I always thought Eddie's comedy was mean. I used to say, "Eddie, be a little nice," and that would piss him off.

But Eddie can act. I don't care what people say, the motherfucker is a great actor.

So throwing me and Eddie together, after so much dreaming by agents and studio executives, sounded exciting as hell. The potential had guys in Hollywood putting money down on new Porsches and vacation homes. Then Redd Foxx joined the mix and Eddie's movie took on the air of history. Three generations of black comics looked like the middle of the 1927 New York Yankees batting order.

Only *Harlem Nights* wasn't a comedy, you know?

It was Eddie's movie—that's what it was. I just wish that I'd been in peak form. For obvious reasons, I never felt obliged to inform anyone about the disease, but the fact was, the MS shit gave me a difficult time. It was my secret, and it put me in a dark place moodwise through most of the movie. I finished thinking that Eddie didn't like me.

It wasn't true. But thoughts don't care about truth and shit. They sit up in your mind and fuck with you whenever.

"Hey, Rich?"

"What?"

"I didn't say anything."

Of course, even paranoids have reason to be scared. In March 1990, after cleaning up at the Betty Ford Center, I treated myself to a long-overdue deep-sea fishing expedition in Australia. However, before I even had the chance to set off from my Brisbane hotel, I got sick. Like severe lethargy and shit. Chills, weakness, weird pain. Despite my objections—I really wanted to go fishing—the hotel doctor checked me into a local hospital, where other doctors hooked up to all this shit and told me that I'd had a heart attack.

"I'm glad you told me," I said. "Because I didn't know that. For real."

"We'll want to keep you here for a month," they said. "You shouldn't travel so far so soon."

"I thought the heart attack was a joke," I replied. "But what you said is really funny."

I liked Australia, but if I was going to die, it was going to be in my own motherfucking house, you know? Following an emergency call, my personal physician arrived from L.A., put me through treadmill and electrocardiograph tests, and then accompanied me back home, explaining I'd incurred a mild infarction.

Maybe. But the effects weren't mild. Afraid that I might die alone, without anyone around to love me, I remarried Flynn on April 1. It wasn't hard. Flynn was there. She had my kids. She liked being married to me.

Smart Rich.

How much did that foolish decision cost you?

Can't remember? Does it matter anymore?

No, because we divorced a few months later and then I was just as alone as before, you know?

But I didn't want to be dead without a wife. Honest. If I was going to die, I wanted a bitch there to cry.

I never considered how much I could stand. No doubt the fire, the MS, and now the heart attack had caught up with me, though I didn't really acknowledge it until shortly before I partnered with Gene Wilder in *Another You*. One morning I woke up and tried getting out of bed, by my legs wouldn't move. Not a fucking kick or twitch. Not only could I not stand, I couldn't even fall, and it fucked me up because I didn't feel bad, you know?

"I don't know what's wrong," I yelled at my doctor. "It just won't work!"

"Things like that happen," he said. "It comes and goes. Some days might not be as bad. Other days can be worse."

Rather than dwell on what could possibly be worse, I spent two intensely hard, exhausting, painful weeks learning how to walk again. By the time the cameras rolled, I was on my feet—fragile, wobbly, and obviously not in fighting shape—but I was on my feet. It took regular cortisone shots and steroid treatments from my doctor to keep me going, but I was determined to finish the picture.

Yet toward the end even that seemed iffy. The picture, which was strife-ridden after a change of directors, ran about eight hundred weeks over schedule. By that time, I was exhausted. I never had a conversation with Gene or anyone about my struggle with MS, but it was pretty clear my body was mostly beyond my control. They started keeping a wheelchair on the set.

Finally, my stuff said, "I put up with you this long. But no more, motherfucker."

Gene and I were doing a scene in which we went hunting and I was supposed to kill him after a run-in with a great big bear. They used a real live bear, who was trained, but a big motherfucker none-theless. With claws and teeth. He stood behind Gene, and before I fired at Gene, I was supposed to talk shit to the bear. Now I don't know if the bear knew he frightened people, but he scared the shit out of me.

If he acted up, I couldn't run.

I was dinner, you know.

Even worse, when the director yelled "Action," I didn't move so hot. I tried hobbling around a bit, but my legs weren't operating like my brain was telling them to. Finally the director must've overheard me arguing with myself.

"Run, Rich, run!"

"No, motherfucker. Just shut the fuck up!"

Realizing Richard couldn't move, he came over and in a private whisper asked if I would be more comfortable having a stunt man substitute for me. Momentarily relieved, I said, "Yes, that would be fine." But then the reality hit me. The only comparison that comes to mind is when New York Yankee great Lou Gehrig was taken out of the game. Only there was no ceremony. I didn't have a stadium full of people cheering for me. Just a film set with a lot of folks anxious to get on with their work.

Yet that was the beginning of me not being able to do the shit anymore.

Whether I wanted to admit it or not.

The MS took over.

32

ONE MORNING AT THE END OF MAY 1991, I PLEADED WITH Deboragh to let me stay in bed and skip my scheduled doctor's appointment. At the time, she worked as my personal assistant. With our history of heartbreak, that was less a job than an excuse to be together rather than alone. She knew that I loved her dearly even though I'd been a perfect asshole in the past.

Ornery, depressed, and weakened by a general malaise that had turned my body into a lead weight, I begged and begged to be left by myself, propped up in bed, smoking, and staring at the television as if it was a Valium. Ordinarily, I got my way acting like a child, but that day Debbie didn't buy my shit.

"You don't look so good, Richie," she kept saying. "I really think you need to go."

Both of us knew how much I hated going to the hospital, even when it was for a routine checkup. But I have a suspicion that sometimes I get together with women for a reason other than just the quest of pussy. Though they mostly behave like bitches, they can also be like angels who watch out for Richard.

"Okay, I'll go," I said finally. "Only if you stay with me."

A few hours later, the doctor saw a funny blip on my EKG and checked me into the hospital for observation. If I'd been observing some foxy nurses sucking my dick, it might've been all right. But about four in the morning, I was awakened by a sharp, horrible pain that made my body contort and writhe as if someone was trying to pull my nipple through my asshole. Then the shit all centralized in my heart, and I knew what was going down.

"Richard."

"Who's that?"

"God."

"Go away, motherfucker."

"Let's wrap it up."

"But I got more material."

The hallway flew by. Lights on the ceiling looked like steps leading to heaven (I hoped) or perhaps a Michael Jackson video. People rushed around me. Doctors hurried to explain the whats and hows of a quadruple bypass operation. I asked Debbie to sign papers that would prevent the vultures from eating up all the money. But there was no time. That was the biggest impression I had. Everything was moving fast.

Was I scared? Scared of dying? Shit, I don't know. A nurse sticking a giant needle into my arm. Another, she explained, was going into my heart. Okay, you know? I wasn't there to argue. But whatever drugs they give you before an operation, you don't have to worry. It takes away all your pain and fears.

One minute I was dying. The next, I imagined that Sammy Davis, Jr., was in the room, snapping his fingers and doing Sammy shit while Frank Sinatra sang a classic. Comedian Jan Murray stood in the hallway. Not wanting my life to turn into a fucking lounge act, I told Sammy to go and get Frank. I wanted him to help me get back in the main showroom.

I mean, if not Frank, then who?

"Okay, Bub," Sammy said. "I'll get him."

Groggy, confused, dulled, and numbed by drugs, I came out of the operation believing that some kind doctors and nurses had gotten together and arranged for my hospital bed to be placed in the middle of a blue trout stream. When my eyes opened, I was gazing out on a beautiful scene in the woods instead of a cold and stark hospital room loaded with heart-monitoring equipment. I worked my fishing rod with as much ease as ever, getting some bites but never the big one.

The nurse who wandered in struck me as a nun. She was Sister Rosie. And I spoke with an Irish accent.

"Sister Rosie, don't stand in the trout stream," I warned.

The same thing happened when the shift changed and a guy nurse wandered in, checking shit. I thought he was an Irish priest and told him to get on out of the trout stream. He looked at me as if I should've known better.

"The Bulls are going to win," he said.

I didn't understand at first, but then something must've fused together in my brain, like a missing piece of railroad track, because suddenly I realized that I was in the hospital and that he was talking about the basketball play-offs.

"You mean the Bulls are going to beat the Lakers?" I asked.

Quick cut. I bet him $30 the Lakers would win. L.A. beat the shit out of Chicago. It was the only game they won the entire series. I was happy, man. But the motherfucker never came into my room again. To this day, I've yet to be paid.

At least I was around to collect, you know. I'd entered the hospital for a routine checkup but left with my heart having been removed, flipped over, and attached to new veins that had been relocated from around my legs and ankles. A long, Frankenstein scar ran down the center of my chest like a receipt from the grocery store. I'd been prepared to die. Expected it. But then I realized God chooses the checkout time.

"Hey, Rich, I changed my mind," He said. "You were right. You do have some more material. Get your ass back out there."

"Just don't smoke," my doctor said as I left.

I'd already gone through a pack of Marlboros in the hospital.

"What about the pussy?" I asked.

"Why not?" he answered.

That's what I said, too.

Why not?

Why the fuck not?

33

ENOUGH WAS ENOUGH. IN SEPTEMBER, I DECIDED TO TAKE MY battle with MS public. The nudge came when producer George Schlatter asked if he could organize a special CBS tribute to me, and I agreed. The show brought together Arsenio Hall, Eddie Murphy, Patti LaBelle, and dozens of friends and performers in an emotional look at my entire career.

Until then, MS had been a private matter. My problem. I was too proud to want to be seen as debilitated. Nor did I want sympathy. Nor did I want to discuss any of the shit. I had more than enough problems trying to figure out why the fuck God had decided to give me MS. I asked the question daily. Sometimes hourly. It echoed in my head like a fucking church bell. Why me? Why did you give this shit to me?

But there were no answers.

So either I could drive myself crazy, which wouldn't have been too long a trip, or I could, as had been my practice since my first misstep in dog poo, milk the entertainment value, sail down the uncharted river of my life, and check out where in the hell the current took me.

After all, I told myself, "Fuck it, you know. This is my life. I've got MS, not death."

Some people found reason to joke otherwise. George had put on a similar event for Sammy Davis, Jr., not long before he passed away. The irony prompted Eddie Murphy, the show's emcee, to wonder how scared I was when George called.

Going into the Beverly Hilton Hotel that evening, I'd worried how people would react when they saw that I needed a cane to stand, that I had trouble walking, speaking, and even doing little things like eating. But at the end of the evening, I was relieved to finally put all the rumors to rest. No more hiding, pretending, or shit, and my bruised pride was mighty grateful.

But it didn't make coping with MS any easier. Each day, it seemed, I was forced to confront the disease. It was like being held captive by a truly nasty motherfucker. One day I would be able to get around using a cane. The next day I wouldn't have the strength to even hobble and would have to use my motorized cart, or "Mobie," as I called it. I spilled drinks, had difficulty eating, and, even more frightening, I once fell in the shower.

Although impossible to cure, I fought the MS by devoting part of every day to some kind of treatment. In addition to the cortisone injections and intravenous steroids that I'd been taking for nearly two years, I saw a therapist, took antidepressants for my mood swings, and worked with physical therapists. I also watched my diet and alcohol consumption.

My doctors said, "You're doing great. You could go on like this for a long, long time."

"Is that a reward?" I asked.

Considering the alternative, I supposed it was.

But even my best efforts only slowed the degenerative disease. That's when I unbaffled this baffling disease. Saw the big picture. Saw it as clear as the first day I got cable TV. It was a message from God.

"Hey, Rich, you ever heard the phrase 'delayed gratification'?"

"Yeah."

"Good. 'Cause you've done had a lot of gratification."

"So."

"Well, now comes the delay."

In some ways, it was more like a total stoppage. Despite two Rolls-Royces and a Ferrari parked in the garage, I couldn't drive a car anymore. I couldn't climb stairs. I couldn't even have an orgasm. But my dick would get hard, you know? Rise to the occasion. Visit me like a friend or something. "Hey, Rich, how're ya doin', brother? Just wanted to say hi."

The motherfucker always caught me off guard.

"Come again?" I asked.

"Shit, motherfucker, I ain't even come a first time."

That's what it all boils down to, right? Can you or can't you? I tried, Mama, I tried. There were times when my dick got hard and I got so excited that I called people just to tell them about it. And the people I called weren't always womens, you know? It was whoever answered their phone.

"Hey, Herbie, guess what? My dick's hard and it's looking at me."

I never prayed in my life, but MS made me pray. I'd be in bed with a woman and I'd start praying, "Please, God, I know you're an extremely busy man. But if you could find it in your heart to grant me a tiny little favor. Not world peace. Not a cure for MS. No miracles, man. I just need my prick hard, okay?"

Eventually, I realized that I should deal with the basics rather than the luxury items—like my bladder. Before MS, I dialogued with my bladder, you know? Like I'd have to piss, but I wouldn't be near a toilet. So I'd ask my bladder, "Hey, there's not a bathroom nearby. You think you can wait till home? Only fifteen minutes or so."

"Yeah, no problem, Rich."

But MS ended all communication. I'd be on the street, talking with some womens, and suddenly I'd start pissing. Feel piss streaming down my leg, squirming into my socks and landing in my boots. It was no different than the other problems I had with, say, my legs. You know, I'd want to walk across the room, but they wouldn't go.

Then the womens, they said, "Don't worry. It's all right."

Clearly, though, it's not all right. I don't like to see nobody piss. So why's it okay for people to watch me piss? And in the middle of the street? But people always say shit like that is okay so long as it isn't them.

Once all the shit ganged up on me at the same time. I was on the freeway, being driven back from someplace, and I was feeling cocky. Somewhere up ahead, a truck jackknifed, causing a monstrous traffic jam. It seemed every car in the world was on the freeway that day. Cars from as far away as Denver came just to clog up the damn road.

As we sat, I saw one of the prettiest bitches I'd ever seen in my life, and she was waving at me. I waved back and the bitch opened her car door, got out, and walked across the freeway to meet me. She kept waving as she weaved a path through the cars. Cute little friendly waves that told me she thought I was cute. Suddenly, my arm started twitching and doing shit, some wild shit, and I tried to get my arm down but it wouldn't go.

"Come on, arm. Quit that shit."

"No."

"Please."

"No."

Just as she got to the car, my bladder decided it was time to go, too. The floodgates opened, the tender of the pump house yelled, "Now!" and I prayed I didn't slide off the seat. She said something about how I was so funny but I could stop waving, you know. I didn't bother to explain. I couldn't. I was too preoccupied. Because while my brain thought about how much I wanted to fuck her, my dick was saying, "Go ahead and try. Ha-ha-ha."

I did what I could. One night I came home and pissed outside because I couldn't get to the door. Right in the flowers. I thought that was okay. In fact, I was grateful to have made it that far and been able to get my dick out. But you know what? The dog was pissed off. He ran across the yard, snarling.

"Rich, man, that's my spot. I been pissing on that geranium for two years. What the hell are you doing?"

"I had to go."

"But that's my geranium. There's a whole yard here."

I gave that damn dog an abbreviated look—ASPCA.

"Shut up, motherfucker," I said. "I may not be able to kick your ass anymore. But I still got my gun."

By the fall of 1992, I was resigned to a life in the slow lane and hopefully few surprises. If I went crazy, it was with my remote control, flipping through 120 channels with the speed I used to drive. But then one day I got my ass kicked. The phone rang. My assistant told me that my accountant was on the line, and he was very worried.

"He says that he heard you were dead."

"Tell him that I was," I said. "But I came back to check the books."

Rumors of my death spread as far as New York newspapers. It's a bitch to be watching the nightly news and see the motherfuckers talking about you in the past tense. Friends called. The weirdest shit was when people who worked for me started to believe that I could go at any time. Like my housekeeper. She'd walk into the bedroom while I was sleeping and start making a lot of noise. When I didn't stir, she squeezed my toe.

"Oh, shit! What're you doing?" I screamed, waking up in a panic of discomfort.

"Sorry, sorry, Mr. Pryor. But I thought you were, maybe, well, maybe you were no longer living."

"Why the hell would you think that?"

"You were lying on the bed. With your eyes closed. Not hardly moving."

"That's how I sleep. How do you do it?"

"But the news on the TV in the kitchen. I heard you died."

"Well, they were lying."

There were probably countless ways I could've dispelled the reports of my premature demise, but the one I chose certainly wasn't the easiest. On October 31, after weeks of working out new material at the Comedy Store, I performed before a sold-out audience at the Circle Star Theater outside San Francisco, my first concert in nearly six years.

Didn't matter how many times I done this before, I was scared, man. I truly was.

First of all, they call it standup comedy, but I found myself having to adapt the format with a big easy chair placed in the center of the stage. Swallowing more fear than I'd known my entire life, I gingerly made my way across the stage with the assistance of a silver-handled cane. Then I sat down.

It wasn't easy. The crowd thought they were there to laugh, but my physical condition also gave them some major drama.

Gave me some, too.

You know?

Afterward, I thought I had kicked ass. The reviews were mostly in agreement.

Encouraged, I hit the road. Although it wasn't anywhere near the same as it had been in the past—none of the drug-induced craziness, the spur-of-the-moment insanity with womens—the outpouring of love I felt was overly generous.

But, after a few gigs, I realized that I had more heart than energy, more courage than strength. Just turning in a decent forty minutes exhausted me way too much. The mind was willing. But my feets couldn't carry me to the end zone.

Knowing I was unable to continue through the early months of 1993, I canceled the rest of the tour.

What a bitch, you know?

It destroyed me emotionally. All the shit that I wanted to say was in my head with nowhere to go. I could hear the applause. I imagined the rejuvenating effect of laughter. There was nothing like it in the world.

34

I HAD MY FIRST ENCOUNTER WITH DEATH WHEN I WAS A KID visiting my grandfather's farm in Springfield. One night he took me for a walk. On the property next door we came across a dead cow. Enormous motherfucker lying on its side. For a moment we thought it was asleep, but it was dead. No question.

Don't know why, but my grandfather handed me a gunnysack and instructed me to kneel down and open it up by the cow's asshole. Then he kicked the cow in the belly. A second later, a possum ran out of the cow's ass. Straight into the gunnysack I held.

"Hold the sack, boy!" my grandfather yelled.

"Holy shit, Pop!" I exclaimed.

You know?

It was a fucking possum! Come out of that cow's asshole!

In any case, my grandfather grabbed the bag out of my hands and swung it over his shoulder, holding it there, despite the possum's squirming, until we came to a big rock. Then he slammed it against the rock, killing the possum.

Okay.

Then I started wondering what we were going to do with that dead rodent.

You know what we did with it? We took it home and my grandma cooked it. We ate the motherfucker. To this day, I don't eat anything with barbecue sauce, because I had to drown the motherfucker in that shit in order to get it into my stomach. But it taught me about death all right.

Life is all there is.

When you kick, that's about it. Show's over.

I'm sorry whatever others may think. But ain't shit happening when you're dead.

A friend once said to me, "Life's a bitch. Then you die. And you don't get change."

You don't get change.

You know that's the truth. The shit they do to people in the funeral parlor, getting you ready for the funeral. If you don't wake up from that, you have to know that being dead means that you are dead. Fade to black, you know?

When my body shuffles off to Buffalo, I want to be cremated. I don't want nobody fucking with me again. Because there are people who like to fuck with dead people. Twist their toes around and shit. I don't want nobody fucking with my toes.

Or my nuts!

On the off chance that I'm wrong about death, I want to make sure that I can still fuck. If there's pussy in heaven, I'll be chasing it. Imagine that: chasing pussy for eternity. Sounds an awful lot like life, doesn't it?

Although death has occupied a lot of my idle thoughts the past few years, I look at it like a report of bad weather. Dark and stormy clouds today. Maybe clearing up later in the week. The truth is— has been and, near as I can figure, will continue to be until the last gasp—that MS may have kicked my ass into the blackness, but I have too much to live for to give up on basking in the light again.

Throughout the illness, the womens in my life have made sure of that. I hear from my first wife, Pat, from Shelley, and Maxine. Geraldine's picture rests on my bedroom table. Flynn comes by, reminding me to exercise. Deboragh, who's remained so under-standing, has never left the spot closest to my heart. And Jennifer, bless her lovely soul, kicks my ass from treatment to treatment and makes sure I get a dose of laughter every day.

Then there are my children. Somehow they've managed to make it in life and turn out magnificently. Richard Jr. continues to keep the Pryor name alive in Peoria while Rain continues to prove herself in Hollywood. Elizabeth is in graduate school. And Steven, Kelsey, and Franklin have their work cut out just trying to grow up in this world.

At this stage of my life, I'm more amazed by their presence than ever. When I look at them, I see so much. I see all my debauchery, but I also see the goodness and the long road of hope and possibility ahead of them.

It makes me love them very much.

Do I have regrets? I think about what might've happened if I'd done things differently. But I can't go back and redo them. So why, you know? What is, is.

I'm glad I'm in show business. As crazy as it sounds, I don't think there are any people like us on earth.

I plan on doing more work—acting, writing, producing. The ideas swirl in my head.

I'm also proud of the work that I've already done. I'm glad I was alive at a time in history when it was possible to record what I had to say, because I think I had something to say. It sounds presumptuous, maybe, a guy from the whorehouses in Peoria. But why not? I came with perspective.

Looking up.

Looking out.

The view was clear. People are nice to each other and they're also mean to each other. That's the way it's always been and probably always will be. The fact that we're different colors is basically just an excuse for doing all that shit. But if people understand the differences a little better, learn to blend the colors, which was my job as a comedian, it's possible to see we're all the same.

Same needs and wants.

A little money, a little wine, a little pussy.

Lately, I've been thinking about something. Back when I was in the Army stationed in Germany, I was in charge of repairing utilities. I was always on the phone, calling different offices. One day I picked up the phone and started talking to this lady who had a nice voice that intrigued me.

A short time later, I got to meet her, and she turned out to be one of the nicest ladies I'd ever met. Although she was married, we used to make love all the time. Mornings, afternoons, nights. Her husband eventually found out. He knew she liked me. But for some reason, he didn't bother as long as I kept away while he was there.

Shortly before I shipped back home, we made love one more time, and afterward she said, "I will come and visit you in Peoria."

Sure.

That's what I thought, anyway.

Then one day, long after I'd been back to Peoria, I was in a bar, and who came in? This lady. She looked wonderful. No different. But I wasn't the same soldier, you know, and it panicked me. I knew she couldn't withstand all the shit in my life. So while her husband waited, I made love with her one more time at the Holiday Inn, and then we said our goodbyes and that was it, the last time we saw each other.

That's been in my mind lately.

Why, Rich?

Well, I've been thinking about where both of us were at that moment in our lives. The future was so unclear. Not bright or dark. Just the future. And our hearts were so strong. I hope that she's all right. I really do. I hope that she found whatever she was looking for.

Life can seem so complicated at times. Yet when you look back what is it besides the accumulation of such encounters with people?

You never know.

As for me, I's amazed that I didn't OD on heroin, get stuffed with coke, or die from AIDS. I think it's remarkable that I'm still here, thinking these silly thoughts. Some people have said it's pure luck. Others say it's testimony to the human spirit. I think it has more to do with something else.

Through an old friend of mine I once said, "There ain't but two pieces of pussy you're gonna get in your life. That's your first and your last, and all that shit in between don't matter. That's just the extra gravy. But you never forget your first and you damn sure won't forget your last. And if you live that long, you're in big trouble."

I'd rather die of cancer than fuck around and remember my last piece of pussy, you know?

I got some this morning, and right now that's as far back as I want to remember.

Oh yeah, one more thing.

I always remember to keep some sunshine on my face.

Epilogue
by Jennifer Lee Pryor

Life is what happens… when you're busy making other plans!

AFTER NEVER ENTIRELY LEAVING EACH OTHER, WE CAME BACK into one another's lives in the summer of 1994. My previous visit in '92 resulted in a hasty exit, and a vow never to set foot back in his life. But I learned again to never say, "Never"! Richard was quite ill and the locusts were swarming: some had nested in his home and he asked me to come clean up. What he wanted from me wouldn't be easy. I'd been living in NYC with my dogs, I'd published my book, *Tarnished Angel*, and this next chapter in my life sounded tough. I made several trips across country, talking things through with Richard. How would we do what he wanted: to help him get better, stop the hemorrhaging of his finances, and get his business back on track? These were the tasks at hand. Richard's life was always high on drama, but it was now going off the chart: things had gotten serious! He'd been diagnosed in 1986 with MS, and his depression combined with all those locusts was now going to create a drama the scale of which I'd never imagined.

I drove cross-country with a friend – my rescue dog Livia – and her son Emmett, and arrived in Los Angeles, officially back into Richard's life, on July 4th weekend 1994. I moved into a small rental home just down the street from Richard and immediately got to work. Everything in the house was topsy-turvy. For example, there was a gourmet cook who was making elaborate meals and fancy desserts. Only problem was, Richard wasn't eating any of them. The locusts were prancing out every evening with three-tiered cakes and candied hams and casseroles, while Richard was on an IV, sequestered in his bedroom. The day I arrived, one of his hired business people was about to buy some furniture stored in the garage … from one of the locusts. Fuck! "Not for sale, buddy …" You can't make this shit up … the inmates were running the asylum. Chaos reigned. I felt as though I was in the court of King Henry VIII. There were guns hidden everywhere … under sweaters in the closet, under the bathroom sink … and there were inmates counting cash in his office … a quagmire of chaos, chicanery and downright thievery. And to top it all off, Richard was living in a very expensive rental home. Thus, with exorbitant monthly expenses, it seemed, on the face of it anyhow, that his plan was to simply run out of money and blow his brains out. But what he really wanted was for his accountants to be fired, his lawyers replaced, and his life saved. And all I kept hearing was the same damn refrain parroted by all these locusts on the payroll: "Richard's gonna end up in an old age home for actors." I knew one thing: OVER MY DEAD BODY!

Alright then, time to get to work! What was abundantly clear … ABUNDANTLY CLEAR … was that everyone had written Richard off. No one was coming round to visit anymore: there was a deathwatch. This situation demanded clear vision, and I had it: Richard would live and participate in his own life again … and have a grand legacy. I had never stopped loving this man, and now more than ever, he needed me. It would be a Herculean task, but I would rise to the occasion.

"Fire everyone. Everyone!" Richard had given me instructions: get rid of the lawyers, the business managers, the works. Spanish maids threatened my life, as did ex-wives and girlfriends. It turned out that nobody wanted to go! We had to obtain at least two restraining orders to keep ourselves safe. Given Richard's new financial situation, we also had to lower child support, and had to go to court to achieve this. But then Richard's grown-up children also caused problems. Richard hadn't been a good father, and his relationships with his kids existed primarily through checks. And so, when the gifts and checks stopped, the problems began, and they're still going on now. I sincerely hope these children, now adults, will get therapy and work through their problems. When they attack me, they also attack their father.

Richard and I remarried in 2001, and this is a wonderful, full-circle miracle. We've had the opportunity to love one another again in a whole and complete way. We have resurrected the good, the magic and the love…and left unhealthy behavior in the past. As Richard says, "What doesn't kill ya, makes ya fat!"

In 1998, Richard was the first recipient of the Mark Twain Award for Comedy. During these past ten years, we have published *Pryor Convictions and Other Life Sentences* (about to go into reprint in England); we have produced an anthology box set, *And It's Deep Too*, and a new anthology, *Evolution, Revolution*; we are Exec. Producers on a pilot for Showtime, "Pryor Offenses"; I produced a special for Comedy Central, "The Richard Pryor 'I Ain't Dead Yet, Motherfucker' Special", and a DVD of this show; and this past year, we established the Richard Pryor Ethnic Comedy Award at the Fringe Festival in Edinburgh, Scotland. But of all these accomplishments, I am most proud of the fact that Richard is alive and with us, lives in peace and with dignity, and has a wonderful quality of life. I also understand I have a mission to secure Richard's legacy and remind everyone who the true king of comedy really was, and still is. We also strive to find a higher purpose for our lives; we have seven rescue dogs and work with different animal rights organizations that champion campaigns on behalf of all animals (Richard has received a Humanitarian Award by Peta for this work). Every day is a struggle and there is an array of health issues, besides the MS, which we have to battle. But Richard and I meet the challenge daily, and I am proud to say, we have grown and love each other the more for it. This man is, and always will be, the love of my love.

www.Richardpryor.com is a website dedicated to Richard and his fans.

Index